SHINTO
WORLD RELIGIONS

by
Paula R. Hartz

☑ Facts On File, Inc.

SHINTO, Updated Edition

World Religions

Copyright © 2004, 1997 by Paula R. Hartz

Facts On File, Inc.
132 West 31st Street
New York NY 10001

Library of Congress Cataloging-in-Publication Data

Hartz, Paula.
    Shinto, updated edition / Paula R. Hartz.
        p. cm. — (World religions)
    Rev. ed. of: Shinto. 1997.
    Includes bibliographical references and index.
  ⌐ ISBN 0-8160-5725-7 (HC)
    1. Shinto—Juvenile literature. I. Hartz, Paula. Shinto. II. Title. III.
    Series.
BL2220.H36 2004
299.5'61—dc22   2004040376

Facts On File books are available at special discounts when purchased in bulk quantities for businesses, associations, institutions, or sales promotions. Please call our Special Sales Department in New York at 212/967-8800 or 800/322-8755.

You can find Facts On File on the World Wide Web at http://www.factsonfile.com

Developed by Brown Publishing Network, Inc.

Photo Research by Susan Van Etten

Photo credits:

Cover: Emperor Meiji viewing farmers harvesting the rice crop near Nagoya in 1868. Collection of the Ministry of Foreign Affairs, Tokyo/Art Resource, NY; Title page: Courtesy of Kohei Sasaki; 3 Jocelyn Marinescu; 7 © Reuters/CORBIS; 12 Hiiroshi Harada/Duna/Photo Researchers; 15 Werner Forman Archive/Art Resource; 21 Izanagi creating the Japanese islands, Kobayashi Eitaku (1843–1890). Japanese hanging scroll, ink and color on silk, William Sturgis Bigelow Collection, Museum of Fine Arts, Boston; 27 T.W. Goodell; 31 Werner Forman Archive/Art Resource; 35 The Bettmann Archive; 37 Drawing, Japanese court life, Tosa School, ca. 1800, Victoria and Albert Museum, London/The Bridgeman Art Library; 43 The Bettmann Archive; 50 The actor Ichikawa Danjuro VII as a samurai warrior, Utagawa Kunisada (1786–1864), woodblock print, Fitzwilliam Museum, University of Cambridge/The Bridgeman Art Library; 53 Portrait of Tokugawa Ieyasu, 17th century, anonymous, Private Collection/The Bridgeman Art Library; 57 The Bettmann Archive; 61 Asahi Shimbun Photo, Japan; 65 Corbis-Bettmann; 69 The Bettmann Archive; 73 Paolo Kock/Photo Researchers; 77 The Bettmann Archive; 79 Courtesy of Kohei Sasaki; 81 Chad Ehlers/International Stock Photo; 85 Japan National Tourist Office, NY; 87 Joe Viesti/Viesti Associates; 89 Martha Cooper/Viesti Associates; 93 Ron Behrmann/International Stock Photo; 97 T.W. Goodell; 100 Martha Cooper/Viesti Associates; 104–105 T.W. Goodell; 109 SCALA/Art Resource; 113 © Royalty Free/CORBIS; 116 Jocelyn Marinescu; 120 John Dakers: Eye Ubiquitous/CORBIS.

Printed in the United States of America

VB PKG 10 9 8 7 6 5 4 3 2 1

This book is printed on acid-free paper.

TABLE OF CONTENTS

Preface

We live in what is sometimes described as a "secular age," meaning, in effect, that religion is not an especially important issue for most people. But there is much evidence to the contrary. In many societies, including the United States, religion and religious values shape the lives of millions of individuals and play a key role in politics and culture as well.

The World Religions series, of which this book is a part, is designed to appeal to both students and general readers. The books offer clear, accessible overviews of the major religious traditions and institutions of our time. Each volume in the series describes where a particular religion is practiced, its origins and history, its central beliefs and important rituals, and its contributions to world civilization. Carefully chosen photographs complement the text, and a glossary and bibliography are included to help readers gain a more complete understanding of the subject at hand.

Religious institutions and spirituality have always played a central role in world history. These books will help clarify what religion is all about and reveal both the similarities and differences in the great spiritual traditions practiced around the world today.

■ Areas where Shinto is a major influence

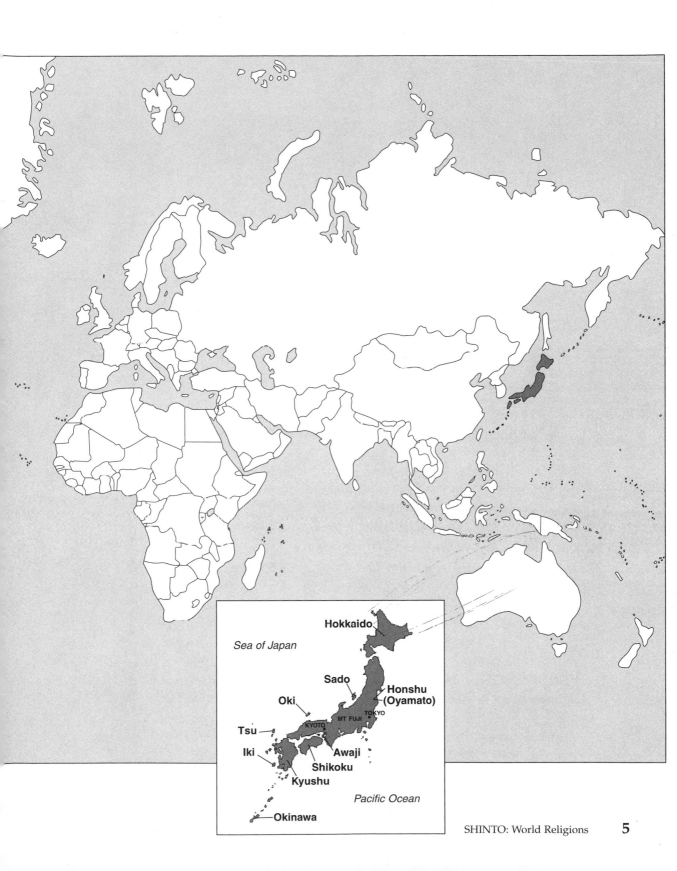

Sea of Japan

Hokkaido

Sado

Oki

Honshu
(Oyamato)

Tsu

MT FUJI

TOKYO

KYOTO

Iki

Awaji

Shikoku

Kyushu

Pacific Ocean

Okinawa

CHAPTER 1

Introduction: Shinto and Japanese Life

Shinto is Japan's native religion. It developed in prehistoric times on the Japanese islands, and it is deeply etched in the minds and hearts of the Japanese people. Because of its close association with the land's geography and history, Shinto is very nearly synonymous with the Japanese character. It has both shaped and been shaped by all of Japanese culture.

Of the slightly more than 127,000,000 Japanese, according to the statistics of the Agency for Cultural Affairs for 2003, 49.7 percent adhere to Shintoism, and 44.5 percent adhere to Buddhism. Traditionally, followers of Asian religions are inclusive and tolerant of other faiths; thus people may practice more than one religious tradition at the same time. They see no inconsistency in being both Shinto and something else—usually Buddhist. In effect, then, one might say that about 106,000,000 Japanese, that is, more than 94 percent of the population, may be considered in some fashion to be followers of Shintoism. Of the others, 5 percent belong to the "new religions" that will be described later, and the remainder, 0.8 percent, are adherents to Christianity.

■ **Shinto**
*The name Shinto is
made up of two Chinese
words,* shin, *meaning
"divine," and* tao, *meaning "way." It is a translation of the Japanese
phrase* kami no michi,
or "the way of the kami."

神　**shin**

道　**tao**

Shinto has been closely associated with Buddhism for centuries, even sharing its temples and rituals. The Japanese have a saying, "Born Shinto, die Buddhist," which indicates their dual reliance on these two traditions at different points in their lives.

Furthermore, many Japanese who observe Shinto practices and worship at Shinto shrines say they are "not religious," or think of themselves as belonging exclusively to another faith, such as Buddhism or Christianity.

What Is Shinto?

Shinto is the Chinese name for the Japanese phrase *kami no michi*, which means "the way of the kami." Shinto had no formal name at all until Buddhism, "the way of Buddha," came to Japan in the sixth century C.E. (of the common, or Christian, era and equivalent to the designation A.D.), and people found it neces-sary to make some distinction. Before that, the Japanese had sim-ply followed rituals and beliefs that had, it seemed, always been a part of their world—those many rituals and beliefs that had served them well.

To understand the Shinto religion, it is important to under-stand the concept of *kami. Kami*, which is both singular and plural, literally means "high" or "superior." It is sometimes translated as "god" or "deity" but more often as "spirit."

In contrast to many of the other world religions, such as Judaism, Christianity, and Islam, most of which focus their belief on a single, transcendent god, Shinto is polytheistic, that is, it has many deities. The title *god* suggests a division between the human and the divine that followers of Shinto do not make. While some Shinto deities, such as the sun goddess Amaterasu, are referred to as gods, most of the deities of Shinto are simple spirits that inhabit the world along with humans. The Shinto world is a continuous stream of creation, from the deities on the high plains of heaven to the trees and rocks and dust of earth and below. All things may have spirit and may speak in their own voices. Humans are not specially created but are simply a part of the world like everything else.

Kami are everywhere, and almost anything in creation may be kami. Natural phenomena—rocks, trees, mountains, streams, waterfalls, animals, thunder—may be kami, especially if they are unusual or outstanding in some way. Not every natural object is kami; however, in the Shinto world respect for natural creation is encouraged, because even the most humble object may turn out to be invested with spirit.

Shinto has no known founder and no central figure like Mohammed, Moses, Buddha, or Jesus. In some respects, it is similar to Taoism or Native American religions, which also trace their origins to prehistory and also venerate many spirit beings. Shinto does not, however, include the concept of a vast overarching power, such as the Tao of Taoists or the Great Spirit of Native Americans.

Another way in which Shinto differs from most world religions is that it has no fixed scripture or holy book like the Bible or the Koran. It does have ancient prayers, *norito* or *norii*, that were handed down orally for centuries before being recorded in writing. One of the beliefs of Shinto is that special words, properly and beautifully spoken, can bring about good results. These prayers are recited to the kami at Shinto shrines by priests during annual festivals, or *matsuri*.

Although there is no fixed dogma, or body of belief, to which a Shinto follower must adhere, Shinto does provide its followers with a code of values and a way of thinking that is deeply ingrained in Japanese life. Cleanliness and purification are emphasized. The grounds on which Shinto shrines are placed always include running water, often a spring or a stream, and as a sign of respect, worshipers bathe their hands and mouths before approaching a shrine. The Shinto ideal is to lead a pure and sincere life that is pleasing to the many kami.

The country of Japan itself is an important element in the religion. While people do not worship their native land, they learn from childhood to love and respect it. Japan is a country of great natural beauty and variety, from snow-capped volcanoes and high mountains to ocean shores and peaceful inlets. Its trees and rocks, streams and waterfalls, along with its living creatures, are all seen as having a spiritual nature.

Shinto practice began among clans in small farming and fishing villages; thus the religion is deeply rooted in the land

■ *The Torii*
The symbol of Shinto is the torii, *the open gateway that stands at the entrance to every Shinto shrine.* Torii *literally means "bird-dwellling"; its crossbeams resemble bird wings reaching to the skies. The torii symbolically leads worshipers to the heavenly kami.*

itself. As a result, Shinto has never spread far from Japanese shores. Its followers outside Japan are mainly Japanese-born people who continue to follow the religious customs of their native land. Unlike Christianity or Islam, which practice organized outreach, mainstream Shinto has never sent out missionaries to spread the faith or attempted to convert nonbelievers, although some modern-day Shinto sects welcome converts.

As a rule, people do not join Shinto in any formal way. They are born to it and grow up in it, learning to identify themselves as followers of Shinto in much the same way they identify with their family, their town, their island, or their country. Throughout their lives, whether they consider themselves religious or not, the followers observe Shinto festivals and follow Shinto practices.

The Varieties of Shinto

Throughout Japanese history, Shinto has readily adapted itself to conditions and to the needs of its followers. When Chinese religions came to Japanese shores around 200 C.E., Shinto incorporated aspects of Taoism and Confucianism. From the seventh century to the mid-nineteenth century, Shinto was so closely allied with Buddhism that it almost disappeared. It has always reasserted itself, however. Like the Japanese people, the religion has adapted to circumstance and changed with new influences and with time. It continues to do so today.

State Shinto

After centuries of being overshadowed by Buddhism, Shinto rebounded as a separate entity in the late 1800s under Emperor Meiji. He encouraged Shinto worship and used government money to support Shinto shrines and priests. The form of Shinto that developed under Meiji's reform was known as State Shinto. It stressed patriotism and obedience to the emperor as the descendant and representative of the gods. State Shinto lasted until the end of World War II in 1945, when it was officially abolished by the government, then under occupation by the Allied powers after Japan's surrender.

Sect Shinto

While State Shinto was emerging under Emperor Meiji, a religious renaissance was taking place, mostly among the peasants and farmers. These people began to follow charismatic leaders who drew their teachings from Shinto, Buddhism, folk religion, and other traditions. These leaders, called living kami, and their so-called New Religions established large followings. Although the New Religions differed in many ways from traditional Shinto, their similarities allowed them to be known as Sect Shinto. Of the thirteen recognized Shinto sects, the largest and best known is Tenrikyo and it is still attracting followers.

Shrine Shinto

Shrine Shinto arose after World War II, when Japan's new constitution guaranteed freedom of religion and barred the government from supporting Shinto as a state religion, and the agency that had administered shrine finances and other business was dissolved. There were more than eighty thousand shrines, the sacred structures where people went to worship the kami, spread across Japan, and with their country ravaged by war, people felt the need of faith. In order to keep their shrines going, priests and other shrine leaders banded together in an organization called the Association of Shrine Shinto. Today, the association oversees the upkeep of shrines, the training of priests, and the calendar of religious festivals.

In the Shinto religion, Japan's emperor has long been revered as the keeper of the faith. The imperial palace grounds contain three special shrines at which the emperor himself worships. The imperial family also maintains a special relationship with the shrine to the sun goddess at Ise, Japan, the holiest of Shinto shrines. At festival times, the emperor sends special offerings to that shrine, often with a member of the imperial family as his representative. Traditionally, a female family member serves as high priestess there, and important announcements regarding the imperial family are made there. The tradition that links the emperor and the Shinto religion is called Imperial Household Shinto.

Folk Shinto

Many people who practice Shinto, however, do so without belonging to an organized shrine. At small, independent, local shrines, and at home, they follow the customs of their forebears, worshiping local kami of the home and the farm. Their form of

■ *Shinto festivals often include a parade, in which young men carry mikoshi, or portable shrines, around the town precincts. The procession takes the local kami, who are believed to be inside the mikoshi, to all parts of the area under their guidance and care and allows the people to show reverence to their tutelary kami. This procession with mikoshi from the Tsurugaoka-hachimangu Shrine is part of the Kamakura Festival in April.*

religion is known as Folk Shinto. It preserves the traditions of Shinto as it was practiced centuries ago and from which come present-day beliefs and practices. Although people who cling to folk beliefs may also be members of an organized Shinto shrine, the heart of their worship is personal. Above all, Shinto is family centered. Many people practice domestic Shinto, maintaining a home altar to the kami and following simple prayer rituals on a regular basis.

Shinto in Japanese Life

Shinto stresses purity and uprightness. As children mature, they are taught to listen to the dictates of the heart; to respect their ancestors, their leaders, and the natural world; and to show gratitude to the kami for the many blessings that they have received. This is the essence of Shinto.

Originally a religion of rural places, Shinto has adapted along with its people to modern society. In some cases, industries have taken on the role once held by small local communities, even constructing shrines on company property. Shinto traditions of being pure and honorable in dealings with others serve the business community well. City worshipers now petition kami once associated with fields and streams for good grades and success in their work.

In this most industrialized nation of Asia, Shinto continues to connect the people to their land by creating an appreciation of nature. The tourist industry thrives on taking Japanese travelers on day trips to Shinto shrines and to the natural wonders long associated with Japan's kami.

According to Japanese lore, the beautiful islands of Japan, with their snow-capped mountains and sparkling shores, their waterfalls and lush vegetation, were created by heavenly kami who then peopled the islands with their descendants. Although few modern-day Japanese people accept Shinto beliefs literally, they continue to express respect and gratitude to the kami who are traditionally believed to have created their land and its people.

CHAPTER 2

The Mythic Origins of Shinto: The *Kojiki* and the *Nihongi*

Although Shinto does not have a sacred scripture like the Bible or the Koran, it does have two highly revered texts whose origins date back to the eighth century C.E. At that time, Emperor Temmu was concerned that the already ancient stories of the celestial origins of the imperial line and the Japanese people were being forgotten and might be lost. Temmu ordered the ancient stories committed to memory. The job fell to one of his servants, Hiyeda no Are. She learned by heart "the successions of emperors" and "the ancient traditions of the past ages."

Temmu's successor, Empress Gemmyo, ordered that the oral histories be written down. The first volume, the *Kojiki*, or "Record of Ancient Matters," was begun under her reign, in 712 C.E., to trace the succession of emperors. The *Nihongi*, or *Nihon Shoki*, "Chronicles of Japan," completed around 720, tells the story of the divine origins of Japan.

These two books laid the foundation for all Shinto beliefs and customs. Other books, detailing the actions of the many Shinto kami, appeared later. The first ten books of the *Engishiki*, a compilation of Shinto ceremonies dated to 927, are devoted to the kami and their stories.

The versions of the Shinto tales in the different books vary slightly, in much the same way that a story may differ in each Gospel of the Bible. Yet the essential messages are the same.

Shinto's rich mythology tells the story of the heavenly and earthly kami and the creation of the Japanese islands and all creatures and beings on them. It also explains such natural phenomena as night and day and answers questions traditionally answered by religions, such as why there is death and suffering in the world. Significantly for the Japanese, it establishes the divine origin of the line of emperors, tracing their ancestry to the sun goddess Amaterasu O-Mikami herself.

The Creation of Japan's Islands

According to Shinto belief, the universe was not created but simply always existed. In its earliest stage, it was an unformed, oily, reedy sea. Eventually, the sea divided into three parts: the sky, or heaven; a middle level, still covered by sea, which would become the earth; and Yomi-tsu-kuni, the land of darkness.

As the universe divided, three invisible kami beings arose from the sea and found their way to the high plains of heaven, the broad expanses of sky above the earth. There they remained, giving birth to other invisible deities. After several generations of being born one by one, the heavenly kami were born in pairs, always a male and a female.

The fifth pair of kami to be born were Izanagi and Izanami, a heavenly brother and sister who had more or less human form. This pair had a special destiny. The other heavenly kami sent Izanagi and Izanami down from the heavens to bring order to the unformed world below. They became the creators of Japan.

Izanagi and Izanami descended by way of the Rainbow Bridge of Heaven to a point just above the waters of the sea. Standing on the Rainbow Bridge, Izanagi drew his sword and dipped it into the sea. As he pulled it out, the briny water that dripped from it solidified and formed the island of Onogoro. Izanagi and Izanami stepped off the Rainbow Bridge onto the first island of Japan.

Izanagi and Izanami wed. Their fertile union produced the eight principal islands of Japan—Awaji, Shikoku, Oki, Kyushu,

Iki, Tsu, Sado, and Oyamato. Izanami also gave birth to many major kami—the god of the sea, Ohowata-tsumi; the god of the wind, Shima-Tsu-Hiko; the god of the trees, Kuku-no-shi; the god of the mountains, Ohoyama-tsumi; and many others. Izanagi and Izanami were the parents of all of the geography of Japan—its mountains, trees, waterfalls, flowers, wind, and rain. At his birth, Shima-Tsu-Hiko, the wind god, blew away the mists that covered the islands, and Izanagi and Izanami saw their handiwork for the first time.

The Death of Izanami

The couple's last-born child, Homu-subi, was the fire god, and Izanami died giving birth to him. Crazed with grief, Izanagi cut up the young god with his sword, and from each piece arose a new deity.

The grieving Izanagi followed his wife into Yomi-tsu-kuni, the land of darkness. Knowing that she was hideous in death, Izanami hid herself from Izanagi, calling to him from the darkness that she had already eaten the food of the underworld and could not return with him. Izanagi begged her to return with him, and Izanami agreed to petition the spirits of Yomi to make an exception for her. However, she made Izanagi promise to wait and not to try to see her.

Izanagi became impatient with waiting and tried to find Izanami. Instead of his beloved wife, he found her rotting body, guarded by the Eight Thunders and the Ugly Hags of the underworld. Furious that Izanagi had broken his promise to wait, Izanami cried out that she had been betrayed and humiliated, and the guardians of the underworld jumped to the attack. Izanagi fled, barely eluding capture. He flung his stick at them, slowing them down enough that he could escape. Finally he reached the gateway back to earth and blocked it with a huge rock. Thus were the dead eternally separated from the living.

Izanami screamed after him that in revenge for his betrayal, she would destroy a thousand of earth's inhabitants each day. Izanagi replied that he would create fifteen hundred new inhabitants each day, thereby peopling the islands. Life would always outpace death, and Japan would flourish.

The Birth of Amaterasu, the Sun Goddess

Feeling unclean after his encounter with death, Izanagi plunged into the river Woto to purify himself. From his discarded clothes sprang twelve new deities. As he bathed, yet more deities appeared. As Izanagi washed his nose, he gave birth to the storm god, Susanowo, to whom he gave the kingdom of the ocean. As he cleaned his right eye, out came Tsuki-yomi, the god of the moon. As he washed his left eye, he gave birth to Amaterasu O-Mikami. Her name means "The Great Kami Shining in Heaven." She was so lovely and glorious that Izanagi placed her in the heavens as the sun goddess. Amaterasu is considered the highest of the heavenly kami, and in her honor Japan is called the Land of the Rising Sun.

The *Nihongi* tells another version of the story. Izanagi and Izanami, having given birth to the islands of Japan, the rivers, the trees, and the mountains, bring about the birth of Amaterasu and place her in the sky to rule the lands. Izanami next gives birth to Tsuki-yomi, the moon goddess, and lastly to Susanowo, the storm god. Many tales refer to Izanami as the mother of the heavenly trio, although others credit Izanagi with their creation.

Ruled by Amaterasu, the heavenly kami lived on the high plains of heaven, a vast area of sky through which ran a wide river that we recognize today as the Milky Way. The kami held council on the riverbanks and decided the fate of people below. Although Amaterasu herself never descended to earth, other gods and their messengers visited at will. A heavenly bridge connected the heavens and the earth, enabling the deities to go back and forth. One day it collapsed, forming the isthmus, or narrow strip of land, west of Kyoto, Japan.

The Conflict between Sun and Storm

Amaterasu's brother, the storm god Susanowo, was a troublemaker. He wept and blustered, bringing destruction to the fields and mountains of the earth until everything was in turmoil and ruin. Finally, Izanagi decided to banish him to the underworld to be with his mother if he did not mend his ways.

The crafty Susanowo played for time. He begged to be allowed to visit his sister, Amaterasu, before he left, and his wish was granted. Knowing her brother's reputation for mischief, Amaterasu asked him for a sign of good faith. As the supreme heavenly kami, Amaterasu knew she could create deities at will. Could Susanowo? They agreed on a test. Each would attempt to create new deities. If Susanowo could create male deities, Amaterasu would accept his word and let him into her kingdom. If he failed, he would have to return to earth.

First Amaterasu broke Susanowo's sword into pieces and ate them. She spat out a mist that became three new female deities. Then she gave Susanowo a string of her jewels, which he ate, spitting out five new male kami. Amaterasu took the creation of these deities as proof of Susanowo's good intent. She presented him with the three deities of her own making and admitted him to her realm.

No sooner was Susanowo there than he began to bedevil Amaterasu and her kingdom. He tore down trees. He broke the heavenly dikes and flooded the divine rice fields. He destroyed palace rooms. Finally he seized a celestial horse and skinned it alive, dropping the bloody horse-skin onto his heavenly sister and her ladies-in-waiting as they sat peacefully weaving. Then he stood back and laughed at the havoc he had caused.

Furious, Amaterasu retreated to a heavenly cave and refused to come out. Her action plunged the whole earth into darkness, and evil spirits took over the world.

No amount of coaxing could persuade Amaterasu to return. Finally, the heavenly kami assembled outside the cave to discuss what to do. There they came up with a plan. First they brought roosters to crow, to give the illusion of the coming of day. Then they brought a great tree to the mouth of the cave, and from it they hung the soft white cloth of the gods and glorious jewels. Finally, they positioned a mirror at the mouth of the cave and stationed Tajikara-wo, the god of strength, beside it.

The mirth goddess, Uzume, began to dance. Uzume was not beautiful, but her good humor and merrymaking were contagious. Soon everyone was laughing. The merriment of the gods partying outside her cave made Amaterasu curious. Finally she could stand it no longer and approached the opening of the cave. "Come out and see," the kami called. "There is someone out here more beautiful than you." Amaterasu peeked out, and she was met by her own dazzling reflection in the mirror. Astonished, she stepped outside, and Tajikara-wo caught her. Quickly, the kami placed a rice-straw rope across the cave opening so she could not return to her hiding place, and light came back into the world again. The jewels and the mirror that brought Amaterasu from her cave became symbols of her power and part of her heavenly regalia.

The story of Amaterasu's disappearance may arise from some natural phenomenon such as an eclipse of the sun—always a source of wonder to early peoples. The importance of the tale, however, is that it gives listeners the assurance that Amaterasu, the sun goddess, will never desert them, and that her power will continue forever.

Susanowo and the Magic Sword

The heavenly kami punished Susanowo for his outrageous behavior. First they required him to bring to the council table the objects that symbolized his misdeeds. These were thrown into the sea, carrying with them the evil they contained. Although Susanowo retained a capacity to bring flood and storm, he could never again make the kind of trouble he had caused in Amaterasu's realm. The kami then sent him back to earth, banishing him from heaven.

Susanowo took with him to earth the eight deities he and his sister had created. They descended to the province of Izumo. There Susanowo wandered the earth. Truly sorry for his misdeeds, he set out to redeem himself in the eyes of his sister and father. One day he met an elderly couple and their beautiful young daughter, all weeping. He asked the couple why they were crying, and they told him that they had once had eight beautiful daughters, but a monstrous, eight-headed serpent had come every year and seized a daughter. It had already killed seven daughters, and the couple feared that the time was coming when it would appear and devour this one, their last. Susanowo offered to kill the serpent in exchange for the hand of the daughter, Kushinada-hime.

■ This hanging scroll by the Japanese artist Kobayashi Eitaku (1843–1890) depicts Izanami and Izanagi, the Creative Pair, at the moment of the creation of Japan. As Izanami watches, Izanagi dips his sword into the sea. The drops that fall from the sword form the first island of Japan. (Courtesy, Museum of Fine Arts, Boston)

The clever Susanowo filled eight cups with strong rice wine and left them for the serpent. It soon appeared, its eight mouths spitting fire, and quickly lapped up the wine with its eight tongues. When it fell down drunk, Susanowo leaped from his hiding place and cut off its eight heads, killing it.

Susanowo cut open the serpent's belly. Inside, he found a glorious, jewel-encrusted sword. Susanowo presented the sword to Amaterasu as a token of apology for all the trouble he had caused in heaven. The sword became part of Amaterasu's heavenly regalia.

Susanowo wed Kushinada-hime, and together they had many children who grew up and married local kami and became the ancestors of all the people of Japan. Eventually Susanowo's descendants spread over all of Izumo province. One, Ohu-kuni-nushi, became the powerful lord of Izumo

---

■ **Glossary of Principal Shinto Kami**

Amaterasu—*The sun goddess and the highest of the heavenly kami; she was born from Izanagi's left eye after the death of Izanami.*

Hoho-demi—*Youngest son of Ninigi; he was the founder of the imperial line.*

Inari—*Kami of rice and protector of all food, prosperity, lovers and married people, and restorer of stolen items.*

Izanagi—*One of the Creative Pair. With his wife, Izanami, he was parent to the islands of Japan and many of the major deities.*

Izanami—*One of the Creative Pair and wife of Izanagi.*

Jimmu Tenno—*Imperial name of **Toyo-mike-nu**, grandson of Hoho-demi and great-grandson of Ninigi; legendary first emperor of Japan.*

Ninigi—*Grandson of Amaterasu, the sun goddess, who was sent by her to establish her government on earth.*

Oho-kuni-nushi—*Descendant of Susanowo; powerful lord of Izumo Province who ceded his land to Ninigi to establish an earthly kingdom.*

Susanowo—*The storm god; born from Izanagi's nose after the death of Izanami.*

Uzume—*The mirth goddess whose humorous dance enticed Amaterasu from the cave of darkness.*

Yomi, *or **Yomi-tsu-kuni**—Land of darkness; the Shinto kingdom of death; the underworld.*

The Establishment of the Imperial Line

As told in the *Nihongi*, most of the activities of the kami took place in the heavens, where Amaterasu reigned supreme. Other deities visited earth for short periods of time, but local kami, some beneficial and others troublesome, along with the many descendants of Susanowo and his children, managed on earth as best they could.

Amaterasu, looking down from on high, noticed that the earth was in continual disorder. Most of Susanowo's descendants behaved decently, but others fought among themselves, and evil spirits ran loose. The world was a noisy place, where even the rocks and the trees clamored for their say in how things should go.

Amaterasu decided to take the world in hand. At first she turned to her son Amano-Oshihomimi, asking him to go to earth to rule her earthly kingdom. As he stood on the Rainbow Bridge and looked down, he saw so much clamor and dissent in the world that he declined.

Amaterasu then convened a council of the kami. They sent a messenger, Amano-Hohi, to earth to look around and report. When three years had passed with no word from him, the heavenly kami sent another messenger, this one armed with bow and arrows. The new messenger, Ame-waka-hiko, had no sooner arrived on earth than he met a maiden whose charms persuaded him to marry her. Eight more years passed with no word from earth.

Growing impatient, the heavenly kami sent yet another messenger, this time a bird, to search the earth. Ame-waka-hiko mistakenly shot the bird, which barely made it back to heaven. But the kami recognized the arrow and realized that their messenger, Ame-waka-hiko, had gone astray.

Now Amaterasu sent two of the heavenly kami, Takemika-zuchi, the god of thunder, and Futsu-nushi, the god of fire, to earth. Following Amaterasu's orders, the two heavenly kami went directly to Izumo, where they met with Oho-kuni-nushi, lord of Izumo and Susanowo's descendant, and asked him to submit to the rule of Amaterasu.

While Oho-kuni-nushi pondered their request, his son tried to resist and attempted to take on the heavenly kami in battle. In a one-sided fight, the kami defeated him. His sorrowful father withdrew to Yomi, the land of darkness, to rule over the evil spirits and keep them from harming the living, ceding control of the earth to the kami.

The two kami returned to the high plains of heaven, where they reported their success to Amaterasu. Once again, she turned to her son Amano-Oshihomimi and asked him to go to earth and govern it. Once again he declined, offering that his son go in his place.

Ninigi, Ancestor of the Imperial Line

Ninigi, Amaterasu's grandson, agreed to go to earth to rule. Amaterasu gave him the symbols of her power—the mirror made by the heavenly kami to lure her from the cave, her jewels, and the sword taken by Susanowo from the belly of the serpent. "Consider this mirror as you would my soul, and honor it as myself," she told him. The mirror thus became Amaterasu's *shintai*, the object in which her kami-spirit lived. Her final words to her grandson were, "May prosperity attend your dynasty and may it, like heaven and earth, endure forever."

With three kami and five exalted beings who served the heavenly kami, Ninigi descended to earth. He went first to the island of Kyushu, proceeding to the province of Satsuma. To the five chiefs who accompanied him, he gave the responsibility of religious tasks. These exalted beings became the legendary ancestors of the families who formed the Shinto priesthood. Each had a special duty. One guarded the chants and prayers; another cared for shrines and ritual objects; a third was in charge of religious dances; the fourth was to make the sacred mirrors; and the fifth, the jeweled swords.

Ninigi fell in love with a young woman of the province and asked for her hand in marriage. The young woman's father offered him instead his elder daughter, who, he said, was stronger. But Ninigi chose the younger daughter because, although she was weaker, she was more beautiful. Ninigi's choice, says the *Kojiki*, is the reason that many emperors of Japan do not live long lives.

The Children of Ninigi

Ninigi had three sons. The eldest, Ho-deri, grew to be a strong man with a violent temper. He had a magical fishhook that enabled him to catch great numbers of fish. One day his little brother Hoho-demi borrowed the fishhook and lost it. Fearing his brother's anger, Hoho-demi sat weeping on the seashore. The sea deity Shiho-tsuchi found him there and asked what the problem was. He advised Hoho-demi to go to the land of the ruler of the sea, Ohowata-tsumi.

Hoho-demi took the boat Shiho-tsuchi built for him and steered it to the sea god's palace. At the palace gate, he climbed a tree so he could see inside, and he was noticed by the sea god's daughter, Toyo-Tama-bimi. She reported the youth's presence to her father, who invited the young prince inside. The two soon married.

But Hoho-demi became homesick, and the fishhook was still lost. The sea god Ohowata-tsumi called all the fish of the ocean together. Finally, a fish appeared with a sore mouth, and the hook was found. Ohowata-tsumi returned the fishhook to his son-in-law, warning him that his bad-tempered brother might still try to harm him. But Ohowata-tsumi promised that he would help the young man by making water flow wherever he planted rice. He gave Hoho-demi the two magical jewels with which the sea gods ruled the waters: one jewel caused water to rise up, and the other caused it to subside. These jewels gave Hoho-demi great power.

Hoho-demi and Toyo-Tama-bimi went home to Kyushu. Ho-deri was indeed still angry, but Hoho-demi used his magic jewels to make Ho-deri submit to him, and he became the lord of all the nearby lands.

When Toyo-Tama-bimi was about to bear the couple's first child, she asked Hoho-demi to build her a private hut where she could be alone. He did as she asked, but while she was giving birth, he peeked into the hut and there he saw that his beautiful wife had changed into a sharklike sea monster. Hoho-demi fled, and Toyo-Tama-bimi, disgraced, abandoned the child and returned to her home beneath the sea.

Jimmu Tenno, First Emperor of Japan

Toyo-Tama-bimi sent her younger sister to care for the young boy she had left behind. When he was grown, the two were joined in marriage and had four sons. The youngest of these sons was named Toyo-mike-nu. He left Kyushu and went to the province of Yamato. There he became the first emperor of Japan, taking the name Jimmu Tenno. Later, he wed a great-granddaughter of Oho-kuni-nushi, one of Susanowo's descendants, so the two powerful heavenly families of Amaterasu and Susanowo were joined.

Jimmu Tenno became the legendary founder of the imperial family. The imperial family has occupied the throne since 660 B.C.E. (before the common, or Christian, era and equivalent to the designation B.C.) and continues to do so to this day. Today's imperial family traces its ancestry directly to Jimmu Tenno, said to be the great-grandson of Ninigi, the grandson of the sun goddess Amaterasu.

Other Shinto Kami

While the heavenly kami and their stories are significant to the imperial line, other kami play important roles in the lives of ordinary people.

The wind fills the void between earth and sky so that the sky does not fall. There are four wind gods—a male and a female and their two kami helpers. Ancient prayers are addressed to the wind kami to keep winds and storms from destroying crops at harvest time, and many shrines are devoted to the kami of wind and thunder. There is also a god of whirlwinds, who must be kept under control so he will not do great harm.

The rain god Taki-okami is a mountain-dwelling kami; Kura-okami is a god of rain and snow inhabiting the valleys. Each takes the shape of a dragon or a serpent. But it is the god of waterfalls, Taki-tsu-hiko, who brings rain in time of drought, and Shinto ceremonies for rain are addressed to him.

Kami of springs and wells make water come from the earth. Kami inhabit the rivers and, traditionally, are continually venerated to keep them happy so they will not cause the rivers to overflow their banks. Other kami dwell at the mouth of rivers.

Trees that have attained great size are often considered to be the dwelling place of the kami, or Shinto spirits, and people worship at them with prayer and offerings as at any other shrine. The trees are adorned with rice-straw rope to indicate their sacredness. This sacred tree is at the Nachi Taisha Shrine in Nachi-Katsurra.

Two major sea deities, Ohowata-tsumi and Shiho-tsuchi, hold the jewels that make the sea ebb and flow. Sailors might call upon them for safe journeys on the ocean.

Kami of the fields and woods are numerous. The kami of fields is assisted by the kami of herbs. But of the earth's flora, trees are especially important. In the countryside a tree may be surrounded by a rice-straw rope to indicate its kami nature. The sacred sakaki tree, *Cleyera japonica*, is often planted on shrine grounds; it was a sakaki tree on which the kami hung the jewels and mirror that lured Amaterasu out of her cave, and sakaki branches are used in some Shinto rituals. Cypress trees, honored for their long life, also grace many shrines. Trees are richly endowed with kami: one deity guards the trunk, the other, the leaves; and before one cuts down a tree, it is traditional to approach Yama-tsumi, a mountain kami.

Each mountain has its own special kami. In summer, people make pilgrimages to the great mountains, either to view the mountains from afar or to climb them. Mount Fuji, or Fujiyama, an inactive volcano and Japan's highest and most famous peak, is home to the kami Sengen Sama.

Rocks, which are great and unchanging, may inspire reverence. The god Ohoiwa-Daimyo-jin takes the form of a rock. Rocks and stones are also the shintai, or symbols, of many deities, including Taki-tsu-hiko, the god of waterfalls.

There are many kami of food, but Inari, the god of rice, is the most highly venerated, and many shrines are dedicated to him. Inari is usually shown riding on a fox, his symbol, and carrying a bag of rice; sometimes Inari himself appears as a fox. As the protector of rice, he is also respected as the provider of all food and of all prosperity. He helps at difficult times of life, protects lovers and married people, and even recovers stolen items. He was long ago considered the patron of swordsmiths; now his patronage is extended to all tradespeople.

The god of sky thunder, representing both thunder and lightning, is called by two names: Kami-nari, "the divine muttering," or Naru-kami, "the thundering god." The thunder god is the patron of bows and arrows, petitioned in times of invasion and threat of war. He also protects trees, bringing on violent storms if they are wrongfully cut. Trees struck by lightning show the presence of kami.

There are also the eight gods of thunder, the Ika-zuchi, who guarded the body of Izanami and chased Izanagi out of Yomi-tsu-kuni. They represent the underground rumblings, such as earthquakes and volcanoes.

The god of fire, Homu-subi, caused the death of Izanami. But although he may bring destruction, he also starts fire for warmth and for ritual. Special prayers are offered to soothe him.

After his journey to Yomi, Izanagi created the Sae-no-kami, or gods of the road. They protect travelers and keep evil spirits away from them. Their shintai is the stick, representing the one Izanagi threw at his pursuers when he was escaping from the land of the dead.

The home is the center of much Shinto worship, so each home has its own kami—the kami of the hearth. There may be a kami of the kitchen stove, a kami of the hall, even a kami of the toilet, who keeps evil and illness away. In Shinto, kami are, indeed, everywhere.

Shinto Mythology and Japanese Culture

The traditional tales of Shinto serve many of the same purposes as those of other religions. They answer questions about the origins of a people and their relationship with the heavenly powers, and about life and death, good and evil. In the case of Shinto, however, those tales bind the Japanese people to their land and to their history.

The mirror and jewels that Amaterasu gave to Ninigi when she sent him to earth are believed to have been handed down through the imperial line. They are said to be enshrined at Ise, the most sacred of all Shinto shrines. Wrapped in silk and sealed in special containers, they are never seen, even by the priests who guard them. The sword of Susanowo, the third insignia of imperial power, also sealed from human eyes, rests in the shrine at Atsuta, near Nagoya.

In the centuries after Emperor Jimmu Tenno, mythical tales gradually gave way to historical records. Yet the celestial origins of Japan and the Japanese people have remained a continuous thread in the national consciousness. The tales of the heavenly kami and the creation of Japan have long been a unifying force for the Japanese people, who have traditionally seen themselves as uniquely blessed. As a people, they trace their existence to the so-called Creative Pair, Izanagi and Izanami, and their offspring. In a sense, the kami of Shinto are their distant relatives, and they feel a special kinship with these spirits of their native land.

CHAPTER 3

Early Shinto and Its Chinese Influences

No one knows when people first migrated to the Japanese archipelago, or chain of islands, and began to make a home there. They settled on the Yamato plain south of Nara, the area identified by historians as the place where Japanese culture began. These people had no written language, so their exact origins are unknown; they may have come from the South Seas or from other parts of Asia. Archaeological evidence suggests that these forerunners of today's Japanese people were a society of hunter-gatherers and fishers. There were native people, the Ainu, on the islands when they arrived, but the newcomers did not mix with them, forming instead their own small farm and fishing villages and settling them with family groups.

Generally, people living in a particular geographical area were related, either by blood or by marriage, and they gathered loosely into *uji*, or clans. They came together to celebrate social events, such as births, marriages, and deaths, and seasonal events, such as spring planting and fall harvest. The earliest records of Shinto reflect close ties to ancestors and to agricultural fertility and the rhythms of the natural world.

The Beginnings of the Shinto Religion

The uji turned to the spirits of nature to be given the blessings of children and crops. They paid respect to natural forces—sun, wind, rain, and tides. Shinto grew out of this tradition, and echoes of it still survive in folk practices, such as the prayers that greet the rising sun. The festivals of Shinto still follow the agricultural calendar of spring rice planting and fall harvest.

Each village and clan had its own local deities, or kami, mostly related to the region's natural phenomena. Living close to nature, the villagers were dependent on its blessings and whims. From Shinto's earliest beginnings, there has been no clear division between religion and culture. People understood that they were continually in the presence of the kami, which they saw manifested in great trees and dark woods, large boulders, mountains, and waterfalls. They paid honor and respect to anything they saw that seemed extraordinary, wonderful, or awe-inspiring. Thus there came to be kami of fire, wind, rain, thunder, springs, mountains, rivers, food, rice, and all vegetation; kami of paths and roads and stones; kami of the sea and the rivers; kami of home and hearth; kami everywhere.

The Norito

Early Shinto did not have a priesthood. The hereditary head of each uji also served as its chief priest. His responsibility as clan chief included being attuned to the instructions of the kami and speaking the words that would ensure their continued goodwill. Shinto followers believed that beautiful words, carefully spoken, had a beneficent effect on the kami who heard them, bringing blessings and prosperity. These mystical words and prayers, called norito or norii, were handed down orally from father to son, along with the leadership of the clan.

The norito, already ancient in the oral tradition when they were first copied down around the eighth century C.E., are the earliest existing record of prehistoric Shinto. Because the words and phrasing of the norito were believed to have ritual power, it is thought that they came down through the ages almost unchanged. Many norito are for the success of the rice harvest, because rice was the mainstay of Japanese agricultural life.

■ *Norito for Exorcism and Purification,*
from the Great Exorcism of the Last Day of the Sixth Month

The Great Exorcism, or Great Purification, takes place at the end of June. It is a ritual to renew the world by removing all impurities and sins. In this norito, as in all Shinto rituals, the words carry great power. Beautiful words of ancient Japanese, recited by Shinto priests, are believed to be pleasing to the kami.

As the gusty wind blows apart the myriad layers of heavenly clouds;
As the morning mists, the evening mist is blown away by the
morning wind, the evening wind;
As the large ship anchored in the spacious port is untied
at the prow and at the stern
And pushed out into the great ocean;
As the luxuriant clump of trees on yonder [hill]
Is cut away at the base with a tempered sickle, a sharp
sickle—
As a result of the exorcism and purification,
There will be no sins left.
They will be taken into the great ocean
By the goddess called Se-ori-tu-hime,
Who dwells in the rapids of the rapid-running rivers
Which fall surging perpendicular
From the summits of the high mountains and the
summits
of the low mountains.

from *Norito—A New Translation of the Ancient Japanese Ritual Prayers,* translated by Donald L. Philippi (ca. 1990, Princeton University Press). Reprinted in *Japanese Religions Past and Present,* by Ian Reader, Esben Endreasen, and Finn Stefansson. Honolulu: University of Hawaii Press, 1993, pp. 90–91.

Characteristics of Early Shinto

The ritual year in Shinto followed the farming cycle. Although different villages might celebrate at slightly different times, in general the people came together to celebrate spring planting, fall harvest, the new year, and events in between and to ask for aid or give thanks for blessings. At each festival, people gathered to ask that their sins be taken away and that they be made pure, to request blessings, and to thank the kami for their goodness toward their village or region.

■ *Following page-Jimmu Tenno, believed to be the first emperor of Japan and founder of the imperial line that has occupied the throne to this day, is pictured here, driving the native people, the Ainu, from the islands of Japan in 660 B.C.E.*

In addition to the heavenly kami, the local kami, and the kami of nature being venerated, ancestors, outstanding people, and the imperial family came to be considered kami as well, so that the pantheon, or collection of all Shinto deities, eventually swelled to about eight million. Many of these kami were tutelary deities; that is, they were the special kami of a particular village, region, or even household, and thus not universally worshiped or even known outside their own precincts. Each village had boundary deities at its entrance and a town or village shrine where people gathered to pay their respects to clan kami, those deities under whose special protection they lived. In addition, there might be other sacred sites for particular kami: a waterfall, a hill, a place where a kami had appeared or where kami presence had been experienced.

The Sacred Places of Early Shinto

At first, there were no shrines or temple buildings. People worshiped in natural places that had kami presence—at waterfalls and on mountaintops, beneath great trees, beside majestic rocks, on the shore—and they marked these places with ropes of rice-straw, signifying their kami nature. To these places the people brought objects, such as mirrors, jewels, and swords, that they felt captured the mystical presence of the kami. Later, they began to build small, simple structures in the style of their own homes and storage buildings as shrines to which the kami might be summoned. Shinto shrines were never built as gathering places where worshipers could assemble. They were for the use of the kami only. Rituals at which people gathered were held out of doors, not inside the shrines.

The Growth of the Clans

In the centuries before 600 B.C.E., the clans grew and strengthened their influence. The uji consolidated, with the larger, more powerful clans absorbing the smaller, weaker ones. When one clan took over another, its guardian kami became the other clan's kami as well, and people turned to worship the deity of their leaders. Amaterasu, the sun goddess, was originally the tutelary deity of the Yamato clan, from which the imperial line emerged. As that clan grew in power and prestige, Amaterasu was elevated to the position of supreme heavenly kami of the entire country of Japan.

According to tradition, Jimmu Tenno, the legendary first emperor of Japan, arrived among the uji around 660 B.C.E., driving the Ainu from the Yamato region of central Japan and becoming the clans' priest and ruler. By the end of the second century C.E., the imperial system was well established, with powerful clan rulers paying homage to an emperor who presided over the imperial court.

Most Japanese, however, were little affected by the doings of the court. They lived as peasants, farming or fishing as their ancestors had before them, paying their respects to the tutelary kami of their own village and shrine.

The Arrival of Chinese Culture

Not far from Japan's shores lay China, with its ancient and highly developed culture. During the Han Dynasty (220 B.C.E. to 206 C.E.), China invaded and colonized Korea, bringing Chinese influence even closer to Japan. From as early as 57 C.E., Chinese scholars and artisans traveled to Japan at the invitation of the Japanese court. Then around 200 C.E., the Chinese moved into Japan, bringing their culture with them.

Japan at the time was still quite primitive. It had no writing system and therefore no recorded poetry or literature. It had crafts but little graphic art (drawing or painting) and no centralized government—all things that China had had for more than two thousand years.

The written word was one of the most important cultural advances to come from China to Japan. Gradually the Japanese adopted the Chinese writing system, fitting it to their own language. This advance eventually enabled them to write down the oral history of their country and the basis of the Shinto religion. But in addition to the written word, the Chinese brought something that had a profound effect on Japan: their religions. In China, Confucianism and Taoism were then already more than seven hundred years old and were highly developed religious traditions. Each would influence Shinto in its own way.

Confucianism

The refined and orderly Confucian system had a powerful influence on the Japanese people. With its emphasis on proper relationships between people, respect for ancestors, and order and moderation, Confucianism appealed greatly to the Japanese court. Confucianism taught that everything in nature, of which people are a part, had its place. Therefore, each person, too, had a place in one of the five human relationships: three within the family and two without. According to Confucianism, harmony in families, in society, and finally between earth and heaven came from the proper observance of these five relationships: parent to child, husband to wife, older brother to younger brother, friend to friend, and ruler to subject.

In the Confucian system, each person had a duty to the other, and specific rules of conduct and courtesy governed a

■ *Court life in early Japan was elegant and refined. This drawing from a series illustrating the life and pastimes of the Japanese court is from the Tosa School, ca. 1800.*

relationship. For example, in the parent-to-child relationship, parents had a duty to love and care for their child, and the child had a duty to love and be obedient to his or her parents, both in life and after death. The relationship of ruler to subject was similar. Husbands and wives had a duty to live harmoniously, and friends had a duty to be honest and fair in their dealings with one another.

Confucianism held intelligence and learning in high regard. Because education was mainly a Confucian ideal, the Chinese teachers from whom the Japanese elite learned reading and writing were Confucian. As they learned writing, the Japanese naturally acquired the Confucian world-view and the philosophy of its teachers.

In Confucianism, the Japanese recognized truths inherent in Shinto. Honesty, fairness, harmony, and ancestor worship were all Shinto ideals. The Confucian emphasis on family, too, was familiar and helped to reinforce the importance of the imperial line. The Japanese adopted many of the Confucian principles, particularly the familial duties, while retaining their belief in the kami and worshiping at Shinto shrines.

Taoism

Although Confucianism was the dominant religious and philosophical tradition of China, China's other religious tradition, Taoism, was also strong, especially among the laboring classes. So along with Confucianism, the Chinese brought their Taoist beliefs to Japan. Taoism emphasized being in harmony with the flow of the universe. Like Shinto, it regarded nature with respect.

Taoism's focus on the *Tao*, the great force behind all things in the universe, and its contemplative side had little impact on the Japanese mind of the time. But the practice of "religious" Taoism, which, like Shinto, had folk origins, fit in well with Shinto belief. Taoism never had the effect on Japanese life that Confucianism had, but it did influence Shinto belief and practice in more subtle ways.

Taoism was more highly developed than was Shinto. It had more ritual and customs than Shinto did. It had a variety of gods who represented natural phenomena, much like Shinto, and some of those gods were incorporated into the Japanese pantheon. Taoism was also concerned with an intricate calendar of good and bad days, and this calendar become part of Shinto as well.

Taoist practitioners had rituals for interpreting signs, foretelling the future, and choosing appropriate places for siting buildings, practices that were eventually linked to Shinto. By the early eighth century C.E., the Japanese court had set up a bureau of divination, modeled on a similar Chinese agency, to determine lucky dates for governmental events and to interpret omens such as natural phenomena.

Buddhism

While the Japanese government was allying itself with Confucianism and reforming itself along Confucian lines, another religion, Buddhism, came to Japan at approximately the same

---

■ *The Waving Cat*

An emperor one day passed by a cat, which seemed to wave to him. Taking the cat's motion as a sign, the emperor paused and went to it. Diverted from his journey, he realized that he had avoided a trap that had been laid for him just ahead. Since that time, cats have been considered wise and lucky spirits. Many shrines and homes include a figurine of a cat with one paw upraised—the waving cat.

time. That religion was by far the most influential religious tradition to enter Japan from the outside world.

Buddhism came to Japan from China by way of Korea, as Confucianism and Taoism had earlier. The official date for Buddhism's introduction to Japan is 552 C.E., although Buddhist priests had no doubt visited Japanese shores centuries earlier. But some time in the mid-sixth century, a Korean king sent a delegation to the Yamato ruler, asking for military aid. With the delegation came priests in saffron-yellow robes, banging on gongs and chanting and carrying with them ceremonial umbrellas, banners, Buddhist scriptures, and an image of the Buddha crafted of fine metals such as gold.

Buddhism had an immediate and powerful effect on the Japanese. It came to Japan as a mature, established tradition with a highly developed philosophy and elaborate rituals. Its color and pageantry, as well as its ethics, appealed to both the rulers and the masses, and it spread quickly. Buddhist philosophy, particularly the elimination of earthly suffering through awakening to a higher peace, was also attractive to the Japanese mind.

Although it was new to Japan, Buddhism had traits that were familiar to Shinto worshipers. Like Shinto, it had many gods, a similarity that helped to foster its acceptance. Also like Shinto, it did not teach or require belief in a personal god, nor did it offer any creed or dogma that its followers had to believe. Like Shinto, it was tolerant of other beliefs and adapted easily to different situations.

On the other hand, Buddhism provided belief systems that Shinto, with its simple rituals, had not offered, and which people had not found in the orderly Confucian system, with its emphasis on rules for proper relationships between people and on good government.

Buddhism also satisfied an important need that Shinto had not addressed. It offered the comfort of life after death, whereas Shinto, more deeply rooted in naturalism, a realistic view of the natural world, merely accepted death as the end of existence. Following a death, Shintoists purified themselves to remove death's polluting taint. Worthy dead, particularly members of the imperial family, might become kami, but Shinto offered no passage to a better place. Buddhism did, and it had funeral rites, which Shinto lacked. Shinto followers embraced this aspect of Buddhism, along with its philosophy and ritual.

Prince Shotoku and Taika Reform

The rise of strong clan rule had been marked by strife among the various clan heads, with the Yamato clan generally emerging as the most powerful. After the clans gave way to the imperial throne in the sixth century, the imperial line continued to experience conflict within itself. Around 600 C.E., a family power struggle led to the removal of the empress's authority. Her nephew, a young prince named Shotoku, became her regent, ruling the country in her name. In Shotoku, the religious traditions of Japan and China blended to create an individual of great refinement and statecraft.

Prince Shotoku is credited with creating a seventeen-article Japanese constitution. This document, written in 609, blended Buddhist ethics with Confucian governmental structure. More than a statement of law, it was a collection of ethical beliefs by which governmental officials were to conduct themselves. In 645, some years after Shotoku's death, Kotoku became emperor and instituted changes in the Japanese government along Confucian lines, known as the Taika Reform.

Principally, the constitution encouraged people to abandon the custom of having power divided among many clan chiefs, of which some were more powerful than others, and to look on the emperor as the supreme ruler of the land. The Taika Reform strengthened the central government and instituted ranks at court. Its laws controlled Japanese life.

The Alliance of Confucianism and Shinto

The emphasis placed on a strong imperial line by the Taika Reform worked to Shinto's advantage. Confucians benefited from their alliance with the imperial court, and the court was Shinto. The Confucians supported Shinto, and Shinto and Confucianism complemented each other. Confucianism brought education, organization, and a political system to the Japanese court, while Shinto provided the mythological basis for imperial power. Among other things, the government built and maintained Shinto shrines.

It was during this period, in 673, that Emperor Temmu ordered a court historian to commit the oral history of Japan to memory so that the "records of ancient matters," particularly those establishing the celestial origins of the imperial line, would not be lost or corrupted by change. In 712, that history was recorded in the *Kojiki*, the written account of the mythic beginnings of Japan and the Japanese people. It was followed in 720 by the *Nihongi*, the record of the earliest emperors. Together, these books established Shinto orthodoxy and the divine origins of the imperial line and firmly established Shinto as the religion of the emperor's court.

Shinto and the Religions of China

For the Japanese, Taoism's appeal lay in its appreciation of nature and its many deities, closely paralleling Shinto beliefs, and from it they took its practices of divining the future. Confucianism stressed respect for ancestors and order, which had been Shinto ideals, but it had evolved into an orderly bureaucratic system of government that was practical and efficient. The Japanese eventually adopted this Confucian model and incorporated it into their Shinto system, along with its code of ethics. Buddhism had many aspects in common with Shinto, but it offered more color and ceremony as well as philosophical depth, and had wide appeal for Shinto followers.

Shinto took on characteristics of the competing religions. During the time that the capital was at Nara, 644–764, the emphasis on Shinto rites in a natural setting gave way to the idea that the shrine was the home of the kami. A form of Shrine Shinto emerged, in which priests performed rites as if the kami were present. A *shimpo*, or divine treasure, was placed in the shrine to signify the presence of kami. The treasure was often swords; archery equipment, such as a bow and arrows, arm guards, and quiver; ceremonial clothing; and harps and bells made by the finest artisans. Every twenty years, the shrine was rebuilt with new materials and the divine treasure renewed. The old treasures and materials were ceremoniously buried on shrine grounds.

CHAPTER **4**

Japanese Religion in Medieval Times

From its earliest beginnings, Shinto had always been concerned with earthly life. The introduction of Buddhism brought notions of the end of earthly suffering and an awakening to a higher plane of consciousness. These were exciting new ideas to the Japanese, and from its introduction, Buddhism found fertile ground for growth. The form of Buddhism that came to Japan was known as Mahayana Buddhism, which liberally interpreted the Buddha's teachings, making it easier for Buddhism to adapt to Japanese ways.

The Teachings of Buddha

Buddhism originated in India around the sixth century B.C.E. According to legend, a young Indian prince, Siddhartha Gautama, later known as Sakyamuni, who had been carefully protected by his loving family from the cares of the world, suddenly became aware of the suffering around him. He vowed to find the cause and solution for worldly sorrow and pain.

Gautama left his family to join a group of Hindu believers, but his new life did not reveal the answers he sought. He left the Hindus and sat beneath a tree to meditate. Many temptations

later, he came to an understanding that human suffering came from desire. Having defeated desire and achieved inner harmony, he became Buddha, the Enlightened One. Buddha gathered followers and preached his message of Four Noble Truths and the Eightfold Path.

Buddha's Four Noble Truths were these:

- Suffering consists of disease, old age, and death; of separation from those we love; of craving what we cannot obtain; and of hating what we cannot avoid.

- All suffering is caused by desire and the attempt to satisfy our desires.

- Therefore, suffering can be overcome by ceasing to desire.

- The way to end desire is to follow the Eightfold Path.

The Eightfold Path was a series of eight stages that led a Buddhist follower to the end of desire. The stages on the Eightfold Path were these:

- Right opinion
- Right livelihood
- Right intentions
- Right effort
- Right speech
- Right mindfulness
- Right conduct
- Right concentration

Buddha's rules for living were simple enough to be readily understood, but they were deceptively difficult to achieve. The early steps on the path were fairly easy for people to follow, but in the later stages, the path grew progressively more difficult. It required that followers conquer all evil thoughts and actions, keeping only good in their minds and hearts, something that could be accomplished only through great discipline and determination. Yet the clarity and simplicity of the eight stages of the path held out the hope that they could be achieved by anyone who was willing to strive for them, a key to Buddhism's great popular appeal.

Buddha also cautioned his followers to avoid extremes, either in pleasure-seeking or in severe self-denial, and to take the path of moderation, another ideal that people found appealing.

Since pain and suffering in life were caused by desire, people could reach *nirvana*, a higher state of consciousness or enlightenment, by controlling desire for earthly things. Meditation was the way to control desire. Buddhism also offered life after death through reincarnation. This tenet of Buddhism held that people may have to live through several lives, with each life controlled by *karma*, or fate. A person's karma determined rewards or punishments according to past lives.

Buddhism Spreads

Buddhism spread quickly beyond India's boundaries and across China and other East Asian countries. By the time it reached Japan, it was highly organized. It had a monastic community, a strong philosophical basis, and many rituals. The Japanese delighted not only in its philosophy but also in its beauty and pageantry. The Buddhist temples were a feast for the senses, with chanting, color, torches, gongs, and incense. They quickly outshone the spare Shinto shrines.

While continuing to rely on Shinto to provide a rationale for the authority of the emperor through his divine origins, the Japanese court of the sixth century C.E. embraced Buddhism. It appealed to their aesthetic sense; moreover it was popular among the people, offering potential support for their rule.

By the seventh century, the government required every family to belong to a Buddhist temple and every home to have a Buddhist altar. Every province was required to have a sixteen-foot image of the Buddha and to support the building of Buddhist monasteries and seven-storied pagodas, temples built like multi-level towers.

Shinto altars remained, however, and the two religions began a long and close relationship, with people celebrating local Shinto festivals as well as celebrating Buddhist holy days and worshiping deities of both religions. The grounds of Buddhist temples, which were large and very elaborate buildings, often contained smaller, simpler Shinto shrines, so that people on their way to worship in one might also conveniently worship at the other.

The union of Buddhism and Shinto in the sixth century is described in the *Nihongi*. According to that source, the Japanese were at first afraid that worshiping Buddhist gods would make the kami angry and jealous. But Buddhism's appeal was so strong that people began worshiping the Buddhas regardless.

Late in the sixth century, shortly after Buddhism had begun to take root, Japan suffered an epidemic that sickened and killed large numbers. The people took it as a sign that the kami were indeed angry. They threw away their Buddhist statues and returned to the Shinto shrines. But soon another omen was interpreted to mean that the kami and the Buddhist gods might work together in harmony. Buddhism returned, this time to stay. By the seventh century it was well established.

Shingon Buddhism

At the beginning of the ninth century C.E., a Japanese Buddhist scholar named Kukai (774–835) traveled to China to study. When he returned, he founded a Buddhist sect on Japan's Mount Koya. Kukai, later known as Kobo Daishi, or the Great Teacher Kobo, taught that enlightenment could be gained through the understanding of Buddhist ritual and doctrine. Kobo Daishi is remembered and honored not only for his role as a religious leader but also for his talents in the arts and literature. His form of Buddhism, *Shingon*, with its elaborate rituals and art, quickly won acceptance in the Japanese court.

Ryobu Shinto

Kobo Daishi also created the doctrine of *Ryobu*, or double-aspect Shinto. He incorporated many elements of Shinto into his teachings, blending the two religions. Shingon Buddhism identified major Shinto deities with manifestations of Buddhas, the many forms in which Buddha appeared to the faithful.

Buddhist scholars taught that the Buddhist gods were the true forms of spiritual reality, and that Shinto gods were the reflection of that reality. Amaterasu was identified with an important Buddha who was originally a sun god. Susanowo, her storm-god brother, became identified with a Buddhist god of love and marriage, a manifestation of the god Bhaishajyaguru.

Buddhist priests served at Shinto shrines, bringing with them Buddhist art, music, and ritual. They celebrated festivals along with Shinto priests and took over the job of performing funerals, which had never been conducted at Shinto shrines. Shrines lost their simple, stripped-down character, becoming more elaborate, both in architecture and in decoration. It became difficult to tell a Buddhist temple from a Shinto shrine. As the two faiths converged, Shinto incorporated many Buddhist aspects, such as loyalty and self-control.

Although many branches of the imperial family tree were Buddhist, Shinto remained the official religion of the Japanese court. Ryobu Shinto, which began in the ninth century as an accommodation to Buddhism, endured into the nineteenth century.

Tendai Buddhism

At about the same time that Shingon was founded, the Buddhist monk Saicho, also known as Dengyo Daishi, founded the Tendai sect at Mount Hiei, near Kyoto, Japan. The Tendai

---

■ *Hachiman*

More Shinto shrines are dedicated to the deity Hachiman than to any other single kami. Originally, Hachiman was the kami associated with copper mining and with the Minamoto clan. When the building of Buddhist temples required vast amounts of precious metals, emissaries of the emperor went to his shrine to appeal for more gold to be discovered. Gold was found, and a shrine was erected to Hachiman in the capital, where he was much honored for the blessings he had provided. The court turned to Hachiman for protection against epidemics and to calm social unrest. Later, he took on the role of war deity and was asked to protect Japan in battle.

Emperor Ojin (ca. 270–ca. 310) was believed to be the spirit of Hachiman reborn into a living kami. Ojin/Hachiman was revered by Kobo Daishi, founder of Shingon Buddhism, and he came to be worshiped in the Buddhist faith as well. Hachiman inspired a great deal of Ryobu Shinto art. By the ninth century, statues and paintings portray him as a Buddhist monk, in an early blending of Shinto and Buddhism. He frequently appears as part of a triad of kami, along with his mother, Empress Jingu, and his principal wife, Nakatsu-himi, who are considered kami as well.

Buddhists believed that simple acts, such as reciting words of faith in the Buddhist deity Amida, could bring enlightenment. From Shinto, the Tendai Buddhists took their close relationship to the mountain on which their sect was located, long associated with the worship of mountain kami. Both Shingon and Tendai Buddhism incorporated elements of Shinto that made them more readily acceptable to the Japanese populace.

■ *Shinto, Christianity, and Buddhism*

SHINTO	CHRISTIANITY	BUDDHISM
many kami	one true God	many gods
purification for impurity	forgiveness of sins	end of earthly suffering through enlightenment
simultaneous participation in different religious traditions	participation in only one religious tradition	simultaneous participation in different religious traditions

---

Japanese Buddhism Grows and Changes

Between the twelfth and the fourteenth centuries, three new sects appeared in Japan. They were Pure Land, Nirichen, and Zen Buddhism. Their founders were originally Tendai Buddhists, but they took different directions. Under their teachings, a simpler, more direct form of Buddhism moved out of the monasteries to the Japanese people.

Pure Land

Like Tendai Buddhists, the Pure Land Buddhists focused their worship on the Buddhist god Amida. The sect was simplicity itself, requiring only that worshipers place complete faith in the benevolence of Amida. By reciting the words *namu Amida Butsu*, "I place my faith in Amida Buddha," anyone might be reborn into paradise. Pure Land Buddhism became very popular.

Nichiren

Nichiren (1222–1281) was a Buddhist reformer who wanted to eliminate all other forms of Buddhism. He preached that Japan could become an earthly paradise, if people followed his way and his way only, to the benefit of both the individual and the state. Nichiren taught that the phrase *namu Myho Rengekyo*, "I place my faith in the Lotus Sutra," would bring about a resolution of problems. Nichiren Buddhism appealed to the nationalistic feelings that had long been fostered by Shinto.

Zen Buddhism and Shinto

Zen Buddhism came to Japan in the twelfth century by way of China, where it had incorporated many elements of Taoism. It brought the belief that all creatures carry the Buddha nature within them and that enlightenment may come intuitively, through meditation. Its simplicity and discipline, its refinement, and particularly the belief in the Buddha nature of all things appealed to the Japanese, who found in it echoes of the Shinto belief in the kami nature of all things.

Zen Buddhist temples and monasteries, in their simplicity and use of natural materials, echoed the ancient Shinto shrines. In Zen, worship of the Buddha and other gods was de-emphasized; temples were stripped of their statues and trimmings.

By now, Shinto and the Buddhist priests, temples, and festivals had become almost interchangeable, and it was difficult to tell the difference between Buddhism and Shinto. Like Shinto, Zen celebrated the beauties of nature and held people to standards of purity and goodness. The art and culture that grew out of this period—stylized gardens; *ikebana*, or flower arranging; *sumi-e*, ink-brush drawings with delicate shading and simplicity of line; *haiku*, poems that portray a single image in seventeen syllables—reflect both Buddhist and Shinto ideals, and many of the arts of the period are claimed by both traditions.

The Rise of the Shoguns

Although revered by the people, Japanese emperors rarely ruled the country directly. They were often figureheads, presiding over little more than the imperial court. Real power shifted from place to place as various families emerged as regional

■ *This woodblock print shows the Japanese actor Ichikawa Danjuro VII as a samurai warrior.*

leaders. By the time Zen arrived in Japan in the twelfth century, the emperor was a powerless but sacred personage living in splendid isolation from the people and serving as the high priest of the Shinto religion.

Beyond the imperial walls, a fierce power struggle was going on. At the end of the century, the Minamoto clan emerged as the victors in the struggle and they reorganized the government along military lines. The land was ruled by a powerful *shogun*, a title that corresponds roughly to "highest general."

The shogun divided Japan into feudal territories, each ruled by a *daimyo*, or lord, a regional ruler who kept peace with the aid of *samurai*, a warrior class. Japan continued to be governed by military leaders and periodically torn by civil war for the next four hundred years.

Christianity and the Shinto Government

In 1549, during this period of civil turmoil, Jesuit priests from Spain, led by Francisco de Xavier—who was declared Saint Francis Xavier in 1622—brought Christianity to Japan. Although Japan, like all of Asia, had a long history of welcoming and incorporating other traditions into its religious mix, Christianity never truly prospered there.

Christianity was very different from other faiths that the Japanese had known. The Judeo-Christian notion of God and the requirement of faith in a heavenly Father diverged widely from a world with eight million kami who resided in all of the forces of nature. The insistence of the missionaries that would-be Christians abandon all other gods and follow the one true God baffled people who were accustomed to believing in many gods and practicing more than one religion simultaneously. Buddhism, like Taoism and Confucianism, had accommodated itself to Shinto ways, and vice versa. Christianity would not do that.

Initially, the government welcomed Christian missionaries and allowed them to set up missions in the hope that Christianity would help to weaken Buddhism, which had acquired great political clout. Over the next one hundred years, Christianity gained enough of a toehold to be perceived by the officially Shinto Japanese government as a threat. Christian missionaries would go into a territory and attempt to convert the daimyo, who might then order all of the people in his district to become Christians as well.

The number of Christian converts was relatively small, but in abandoning Shinto and Buddhism, those converts were rejecting the whole foundation on which the imperial system and the Japanese government were based. Moreover, the Christians were under the influence of European forces, as represented by the Spanish priests. The government therefore viewed the budding Christian movement with alarm.

Tokugawa Rule

A powerful shogun named Ieyasu emerged in 1603. By 1615, he and his family of military rulers, the Tokugawa, had unified Japan and centralized their power. They moved the capital to Edo (now Tokyo). Under the Tokugawa, Japan would remain at peace for the next two hundred fifty years.

The Tokugawa government required all families to be members of their local Buddhist temple, and temple membership was made hereditary. These policies enabled the rulers to keep track of the populace. People had to report to the temple all births, marriages, deaths, and changes of address.

Along with the requirement to join a Buddhist temple came an attempt to suppress Christianity as an unhealthy foreign influence. This ultimately led to an armed uprising of Japanese Christians. The uprising only served to amplify the government's fears about European tampering in Japanese affairs. Christianity was officially banned. The Christian movement went underground, where it remained in secret for the next two hundred years.

In the 1630s, the third Tokugawa ruler expelled all foreigners from Japan and closed its ports to all European traders. Because they had not tried to spread Christianity among the Japanese, a few Dutch merchants were permitted to carry on restricted trade from the island of Deshima in Nagasaki Bay, but they were not allowed to leave the island except to report to the shogun at Edo once a year. At the same time, laws were passed forbidding Japanese to leave Japan. A curtain of isolation fell between Japan and the rest of the world. This period lasted for two hundred fifteen years.

■ *Tokugawa rule
extended from 1603 to
the mid-1800s. This por-
trait by an unknown
artist depicts Ieyasu,
a Tokugawa ruler from
the seventeenth century.*

Shinto Under the Tokugawa

Although it was mandated, Buddhism never completely replaced other religions in Japan. Shinto kami were worshiped in Buddhist temples, and Shinto shrines still attracted families for spring and fall festivals, new year celebrations, and special occasions such as the birth of a child.

Shinto continued to flourish during Tokugawa times. The Tokugawa government, officially Shinto, was arranged on Confucian lines, and Confucianism and Shinto had long been allied. What came to be known as Tokugawa values permeated Japanese culture. They included reverence for the kami for the blessings of nature, respect for parents and worship of ancestors, and loyalty to the government. Fundamentally Confucian but imbued with Shinto, those values remain the basis of Japanese culture today.

Tokugawa society was arranged in a strict hierarchical structure that stressed loyalty and service to the government. Warriors, because they protected the state, had the highest status. Farmers, who produced food for the people, came next, followed by workers, who served others and were therefore good for society. At the bottom of the list were merchants, who lived by selling what others produced. There was little movement between classes. Most people continued to live by agriculture, farming, and fishing as their ancestors had before them.

Shinto Renewal

The Tokugawa shoguns demanded order, obedience, loyalty, and calm. During the late eighteenth and early nineteenth centuries, a relative peace settled on the Japanese islands. As the period of warfare and civil strife faded into memory, scholars turned their attention to history, literature, and the arts. At first they concentrated on the Chinese classics and Buddhism, but soon they began to study Japan's native culture. One daimyo of the Tokugawa line brought together scholars and assembled the first history of Japan.

Scholars turned next to early Shinto literature, collecting tales and writing them down. The Shinto calendar of lucky and unlucky days, based on the Chinese/Taoist tradition, was

■ Norito for Good Harvest

Not all norito were passed down from ancient times. Some, like this one, were composed later, and even continue to be written today. Typically, this later norito calls on the kami to hear the prayers of the people for help with practical concerns of the time, including a rich harvest and the continuing bounty of the earth.

Now that His Imperial Majesty, about to make the beginning of the rice crop for this year, has caused offerings to be presented in abundance, do we [coming] cleansed and purified into thy great presence, make offerings—of food offerings: soft rice and rough rice; of drink offerings: making high the tops of the wine jars and arranging in full rows the bellies of the wine jars; of things that live in the blue sea-plain, things broad of fin and things narrow of fin, even to grasses of the offing and grasses of the shore—all these do we offer in abundance; and as the full and glorious sun of this day of life and plenty rises, do thou hear to the end these words of praise, in tranquility and peace. [Grant that] all things that may be grown, beginning with the late-ripening rice which will be produced by the people by stirring with arms and hands the foamy waters and by drawing the mud together between the opposing thighs, and extending even to the part blade of grass, [grant that they] may not meet with evil winds or violent waters; prosper them with abundance and luxuriance, and make the Festival of New Food to be celebrated in sublimity and loveliness. Thus, with dread, we declare the ending of the words of praise.

from *The National Faith of Japan,* by Daniel C. Holtom. Reprinted in *Japanese Religions Past and Present,* by Ian Reader, Esben Endreasen, and Finn Stefansson, Honolulu, University of Hawaii Press, 1993.

revived, and Shinto festivals were encouraged. The government still maintained Shinto shrines, and people gathered regularly at festivals to give thanks to the kami for their many blessings.

Buddhist scholars had long taught that Buddhist gods represented divine reality, and that the Japanese kami were their worldly "trace" or reflection. Now Shinto scholars reversed the doctrine, holding that the kami were the true divinities of Japan and that the Buddhist deities were a reflection of them. Confucianism and Buddhism were de-emphasized, and Shinto was once again elevated in religious importance.

CHAPTER 5

Shinto and Japanese Nationalism: 1868–1945

By the mid-1800s, Japan had been effectively isolated from the rest of the world for more than two hundred years. Japanese society was organized along the lines of feudalism, with military leaders holding vast tracts of land that were worked by peasants—a system that had died out in Western Europe some three hundred years earlier. The imperial court had become mainly a place of art and refinement, where the emperor reigned with pomp and pageantry but had little real influence. Powerful shoguns controlled large areas that were administered by daimyo and farmed by peasants.

In Western Europe and America, the invention of the steam engine had ushered in the industrial revolution. People had moved in droves from the farm to the factory; canals and railroads linked growing cities. But Japan's door was closed to nearly all foreigners and the changes they might bring. What trade was permitted with the outside world was accomplished through the Dutch agents on the tiny island of Deshima in Nagasaki harbor. A few modern improvements made their way to the imperial court, but for the most part, the Japanese people continued to live as their ancestors had lived, farming and fishing, mostly in peasant villages and small towns.

Indeed, many Japanese barely knew that the rest of the world existed. Scholars managed to get around the ban on foreign literature, and they learned about the botany, medicine, military tactics, and mathematics of the day. Literacy was not widespread, however. Various reformers did bring improvements in irrigation and farming, though not many.

The Waning of the Shogunate

Japan's isolation delayed progress, but it also promoted a sense of national unity. While the rest of the world went through upheaval and change, the Japanese enjoyed a period of relative calm and, in the ruling classes, a certain luxury. Buddhist doctrine had held that Buddhist gods represented true reality and Shinto deities echoed them. Now Shinto scholars, encouraged by the imperial court, reversed that teaching. They advanced the doctrine that Shinto deities were the true reality and Buddhist gods their reflection. As a result of these changes, Confucianism and Buddhism lost some of their influence. The resurgence of Shinto also brought renewed respect for the emperor, and the once total authority of the powerful shogun began to lose its luster and gradually it waned.

In this long period of domestic peace, the warrior class lost its true purpose. The daimyo and the samurai turned to education and the arts. Among other things, they studied Shinto, learning about the sacred history of their islands and the divine origins of their emperor.

Japan Opens Its Gates

By the 1850s, the outside world had changed dramatically. Steamships were circling the world. Firearms had revolutionized warfare. The invention of the power loom was the starting point for the age of factories. Japan, meanwhile, remained a living relic of feudalism, mired in its own past and turning away any foreign ship that wandered into its waters.

Perched on the edge of the Pacific Rim, an important socioeconomic region of countries surrounding the Pacific Ocean, Japan was ideally located for many reasons. Foreign ships could stop on a long sea journey for provisions and fresh water. Whalers and fur traders could seek safe harbor from the typhoons that blew up unexpectedly in the Pacific. But Japan's isolationist policies forbade those typical "outsiders" from stopping on its shores. Indeed, sailors were met with outright hostility if their ships needed assistance in Japanese waters or if they were shipwrecked on Japanese land. Often those sailors were attacked, or worse, killed, rather than assisted. As world trade grew and more and more ships sailed the Pacific, the situation became increasingly worse.

In 1853, when United States President Franklin B. Pierce initiated negotiations for trade with Japan, his goal was to make Japanese harbors accessible to ships from the United States. He dispatched Commodore Matthew C. Perry to Japan with orders to secure a trade relations treaty with the Japanese government.

After several unsuccessful attempts to present the United States' demands to either the emperor or the shogun in power, Perry left, saying that he would return for their reply. In

---

■ Tanka

The *tanka* is an ancient Japanese poetic form. It has 31 syllables, divided into phrases of 5, 7, 5, 7, 7 syllables. Although often used by Buddhist and Zen poets, the tanka has distinctly Shinto origins. Tanka appear in the *Kojiki* and were part of the oral tradition before they were written down. According to legend, the first tanka was composed by Susanowo, the storm deity.

Emperor Meiji is said to have written one hundred thousand tanka, many in the classic style, with Shinto themes, celebrating the beauties of nature.

> The morning sun
> Rises so splendidly
> Into the sky:
> Oh, that we could attain
> Such a clear reviving soul!
> In the palace tower
> Each and every window
> Was opened widely
> And then in four directions
> We viewed the cherry in full bloom!

> —*Emperor Meiji* (r. 1868–1912)

February 1854, Perry steamed into Tokyo harbor with nine warships and sixteen hundred troops. He carried a letter from the president asking that the ports be opened to foreign trade and that American sailors be afforded better treatment.

Many of the daimyo had planned to resist the American overtures, but Perry's display of might left no room for argument. The Japanese had no choice but to welcome Perry's delegation to their shores.

In the end, the warlords acceded to the demands of the United States. Two ports were to be opened to limited trade, shipwrecked sailors would be well treated, and an American consul would be allowed to reside in Japan. Japan was open to foreign trade for the first time in more than two centuries.

The concession to America further weakened the shogun's power. The more fiercely nationalistic of the warlords still felt that Japan should have resisted United States' demands, while those who had acceded defended their position. Political wrangling eventually led to the downfall of Tokugawa, the end of the shogunate in Japan, and the return of imperial rule.

The Meiji Restoration

In 1868, sixteen-year-old Emperor Mutsuhito took the throne. He adopted the title Meiji and began his rule, like many emperors before him, as a figurehead. His actions as emperor, however, and the series of events surrounding his rise to power had vast implications for Shinto and the Japanese people.

For centuries, Japan's emperors had been politically ineffective, with shoguns doing the actual ruling. Now, however, winds of change were sweeping across Japan. The shogun's power had eroded. As a reaction to new foreign influences entering Japan, Shinto, the native Japanese religion, was enjoying a resurgence. Western trade was expanding. Meiji and his advisers felt that the time was ripe for other changes as well. It was clear to them that they would have to make friends with the United States and with Europe in order to acquire Western technology and become an equal player on the world stage. If not, they would risk being forever backward and possibly falling under Western domination. Meiji and his advisers decided to cultivate

■ *Portrait of the young Emperor Meiji, who in 1869, established Shinto as the national religion of Japan.*

the West deliberately as a strategy for becoming a world power. The young emperor took over the shogun's palace in Edo, and renamed the city Tokyo, or "eastern capital," replacing Kyoto as the seat of government.

The immediate goals of the new administration were to restore the authority of the imperial throne and to return Shinto to its rightful position as the national religion of Japan. Both goals would be served by Shinto worship, which emphasized the divine origins of the imperial line and promoted a sense of national pride and unity that had waned under Buddhism. Revival Shinto was to be the spiritual foundation for the "new Japan" that would emerge under Meiji.

The Charter Oath

The young emperor Meiji almost immediately signed a document called the Imperial Charter Oath. Its articles called for the establishment of assemblies for public discussion of national policy; the inclusion of all classes in carrying out affairs of state; the opening of career paths to all people; an end to the "evil customs of the past"; and, most important, the strengthening of imperial rule. Japan's key to the future would be its ancient and honored customs and beliefs combined with modern knowledge.

Under the Meiji Restoration, as the movement came to be called, a parliamentary system of government replaced feudalism. For the first time, people could choose where they would live. Occupations that had once been hereditary were opened to all. The shogun who had ruled from Edo was gone. In 1869, four powerful daimyo voluntarily turned over their holdings to the emperor. Other daimyo soon did the same. They were given pensions and allowed to retire. The samurai were released from service. Those able and educated men quickly found new outlets for their administrative talents. Many became businessmen; others went into politics. The government inaugurated trade and diplomatic relations with Europe and the United States. Education was made compulsory for all children, and military service was required of adult men. This was a period of intense social change and industrial growth in Japan, and the young emperor's power and prestige continued to soar.

The Establishment of State Shinto

On April 25, 1869, Emperor Meiji, in his role as chief priest, appeared before Japan's leaders. He led Shinto ceremonies, addressing all the kami, and then read the newly issued Imperial Charter Oath, officially making it the law of the land. His actions reestablished the age-old principle of the unity of Shinto worship and government.

Meiji's actions revived "pure" Shinto, which stressed the emperor's divine right to rule and the ascendancy of the kami over the gods of other religions. Shinto was officially made the national religion. Under the new charter, the emperor was venerated by the people as a living kami.

The centuries' old alliance of Shinto and Buddhism ended. Shinto objects of worship were removed from Buddhist temples, Buddhist statues and art were removed from Shinto shrines, and the two religions were required to separate and set up independent places of worship. Originally, the government's intent had been to suppress Buddhism, but Buddhism was too deeply entrenched in Japanese culture. Buddhism was not suppressed, but the two religions officially separated, taking over different shrines and temples and developing distinct identities. Ryobu, or double-aspect Shinto, the combination of Shinto and Buddhism, passed into history.

Shinto in the Meiji Era

Under the new charter, a department of divinity was created. Its purpose was to advance the Shinto doctrine of the divine origins of the imperial line as a rationale for restoring the power of the emperor. Instead of achieving priesthood through heredity, priests were appointed by the government. Most of the Shinto priests who had inherited their positions were reappointed, but now they reported to a governmental agency that had the power to discipline or dismiss them.

One of the effects of making Shinto a state institution was that people began to view Shinto and religion as two different things. The Shinto priesthood had no problem with performing rituals for the benefit of the nation, but they saw this as different from "religion," which they associated with worship, doctrine, rites such as funerals, and prayer. Japanese scholars began to debate whether Shinto was or was not a religion.

The government declared Shinto to be nonreligious, but its observation was made a patriotic duty. Among other things, this fulfilled the constitutional promise of freedom of religion, while mandating Shinto. Shrines were declared national establishments for promoting community and morality, and they were supported by the state. Schools taught National Ethics, a blend of Shinto and Confucianism that included the celestial origins of the emperor and the sacred character of the Japanese nation and its people. Whole classes of schoolchildren were taken to the shrines to pay their respects to their country and their emperor.

The government established new shrines that elevated emperors and members of the imperial family to the level of deities. Emperors were considered kami during their lifetime, until Emperor Hirohito renounced his divinity in January 1946 after World War II. Military heroes were also enshrined. It was considered a great honor to have died for Japan in battle. The Yasukuni Shrine in Tokyo, which enshrined the war dead, became one of the country's most important shrines. The emperor himself conducted rituals there, and fallen soldiers were worshiped as kami. All of these things served to make Japan intensely nationalistic and played a role in the unification of its people during World War II.

Sect Shinto—The New Religions

Many people felt religiously adrift as Buddhism lost its influence and the state promoted nonreligious Shinto. A number of people turned to religious movements that had sprung up in the countryside, mostly among the common people. Some of these "New Religions" traced their origins to pre-Meiji times, and others appeared both during and after the Meiji period. Although not literally new, they were new compared to the ancient traditions of Buddhism and Shinto. Thirteen sects were classified by the Meiji government as Sect Shinto and allowed to continue their religious practices as separate from the Shinto mandated by the state.

Some of the New Religions had distinct Folk Shinto characteristics. Some had evolved from the mountain worship cults, where deities were thought to reside in great sacred mountains such as Mount Fuji. Others concentrated on stressing the importance of purification of water for body and mind. Several combined aspects of Revival Shinto and Confucianism, logically connecting State Shinto with the Confucian ideal of good government. Most, however were basically Shinto.

Finally, there were sects organized around a founder who gathered followers, usually after a divine revelation or ecstatic experience, and made faith healing a part of their belief. Of these, the best known is Tenrikyo, "Teaching of the Heavenly Truth," or the religion of divine wisdom.

■ *Following page-During the period of State Shinto, emperors both past and present were elevated to the level of kami and shrines were built to them. Here, Shinto priests make an offering of tea to the kami spirit of Emperor Meiji during an annual festival in his memory at the Meiji Shrine in Tokyo.*

Tenrikyo was founded in 1838 by a woman from a small village in central Japan. While attending a healing ceremony for her son, Miki Nakayama (1798–1887) had an ecstatic experience in which she was visited by a creator deity, God the Parent, the original parent of humanity. Nakayama became a "living kami." The deity, speaking through her, caused her to teach and preach about her experience, exhorting followers to remove the impurities from their lives and live joyously, helping others. Everything associated with Nakayama became kami. Her life is its sacred model, her writings its scripture.

Tenrikyo doctrine teaches that wrong use of the mind causes illness, and purification of the mind relieves it. Nakayama identified the eight "mental dusts" that caused wrong use of the mind: miserliness, or stingy, ungenerous behavior; covetousness, or wanting what others have; hatred; self-love; enmity, or bitter feelings toward another; anger; greed; and arrogance. Tenrikyo grew rapidly. Followers built dwellings near Nakayama's little village, and eventually it swelled to become a city, Tenri, which includes Tenrikyo church headquarters, dormitories, schools, and a hospital.

Kurozumikyo, another of the older New Religions, was founded at the end of the Tokugawa era by Kurozumi Munetada, a hereditary Shinto priest of the samurai class. Kurozumi, a devout worshiper of Amaterasu, received a revelation in which the sun seemed to enter his body through his mouth, uniting him with the divinity. Kurozumi was himself a healer, and people began coming to him for help. He vowed to teach enlightenment and to spread the way to others. The cornerstone of his doctrine was daily worship of the sun and the recitation of the Great Purification Prayer. Kurozumi developed an organization that included disciples who won converts to him and his doctrine. The sect was officially recognized by the Meiji government in 1876.

Buddhism, too, produced new religions. Soka Gakkai, one of the largest of the New Religions, was founded in the early 1900s, an offshoot of the Nichiren Buddhist tradition. Followers chant the Lotus Sutra, believing that placing total faith in its strength will solve all worldly problems.

The popularity and growth of the sects during Meiji times reflected the needs of the populace for a belief system. The sects differed from State Shinto in that they were "religious" in character, from classic Shinto in that they introduced elements of Buddhism, Taoism, Confucianism, folk belief, and even Christianity; yet most were recognizably Shinto. The sects of Sect Shinto mainly rejected shrine worship, building instead assembly halls that were called churches, not shrines.

army, resentment of the civilian government grew. With military leaders holding most of the positions of power in the government, they began a campaign to bring the whole world under the rule of the emperor. As a rationale, they quoted the legendary emperor Jimmu Tenno: "The imperial rule shall be extended to all the cardinal points and the whole world shall be brought under one roof," claiming that because the emperor had received his power directly from Amaterasu, the sun goddess, he was therefore the only rightful ruler on earth. Japan began an unyielding march across Asia.

In 1931, Japan seized Manchuria, with its rich iron and steel industries, and forced the people there into producing steel for the empire. In 1937, at a time when China was weakened by civil war, Japan invaded northern China. China resisted with help

from the British and the United States, and Japan's attack ended in a standoff.

By then, war had broken out in Europe. Many Japanese believed that Germany would be the winner. In 1941, the Imperial Council voted to go to war against the United States.

On December 7, 1941, Japan attacked Pearl Harbor in the Hawaiian Islands, a United States territory lying in the North Pacific Ocean, thus bringing the United States into World War II. For Japan, this proved to be a great tactical error. The United States responded fiercely. Over the next three years of the war, all of Japan's ports were destroyed, along with three quarters of its naval fleet, and ninety of its major cities were firebombed. Half of all its industry was damaged beyond repair.

The people, taught from birth that their emperor was descended from the gods and that death in the service of the

---

■ Excerpt from Emperor Hirohito's Address to the Japanese People, January 1, 1946

After Japan's defeat in World War II, Emperor Hirohito, in his traditional New Year's address, spoke to console and encourage the Japanese people and to renounce the notion of the imperial divinity that had carried them into war.

...we know that the spirit of love of home and the spirit of love of country are especially strong in our nation. Now in truth is the time for expanding this and for putting forth sacrificial efforts for the consummation of the love of mankind. When we reflect on the results of the long-continued war which has ended in our defeat, we fear that there is danger that our people find the situation hard to bear and that they sink to the depths of discouragement. As the winds of adversity gradually heighten, there is peril in the weakening of moral principles and the marked confusion of thought that they bring.

We stand together with you our countrymen. Our gains and losses have ever been one. We desire that our woe and weal should be shared. The bonds between us and our countrymen have been tied together from first to last by mutual trust and affection. They do not originate in mere myth and legend. They do not have their basis in the fictitious ideas that the emperor is manifest god and that the Japanese people are a race superior to other races and therefore destined to rule the world...

—from Emperor Hirohito's Address

emperor would bring them the status of kami, fought on in the face of ever-lengthening odds. Japanese pilots by the hundreds flew their bomb-laden airplanes directly into their targets and died in the crash. These young men were known as *kamikazes*— "winds of the gods."

In July 1945, at the Potsdam Conference, the United States, Great Britain, and China demanded unconditional surrender by the Japanese or they would suffer "prompt and utter destruction." When the Japanese did not respond, the United States dropped the first atomic bomb on the Japanese city of Hiroshima on August 6, 1945; three days later a second bomb was dropped on Nagasaki. On August 10, Emperor Hirohito broke a deadlock in the Imperial Council by agreeing to surrender, and on August 14, the Allies received word from Japan that it would accept the terms of the Potsdam Conference.

Shinto in Postwar Japan

In the aftermath of the war, the Japanese adopted a new constitution, giving power to the people of Japan and making the emperor a constitutional monarch and the "Symbol of the State." Japan gave up its right to use force to settle international disputes and to raise a military force.

The new constitution guaranteed freedom of religion. Government support for Shinto or any other religion was outlawed. Shinto would survive as the principal religion of the Japanese people, but it would never again be state mandated or supported. In an address to the people on New Year's Day, 1946, Emperor Hirohito renounced forever any claim to divinity.

No longer a state religion, Shinto regrouped. Many shrines came together to form an organization called the Association of Shrine Shinto. This organization coordinates the activities of the more than 81,000 Shinto shrines in Japan.

The emperor still acts as chief priest of Imperial Shinto, carrying on worship at the three shrines inside the palace. The ancient rites of Imperial Shinto ask the blessing of the kami on the land and its people. The imperial line also maintains a special relationship with the shrine at Ise, which is devoted to the goddess Amaterasu, the legendary ancestor of the emperor.

CHAPTER **6**

Shinto Belief and Ritual

Shinto is often described as a happy religion. It assumes a basic goodness in people and in the universe. Its believers express their religion joyously in festivals that bring people together for worship and celebration. Unlike the Judeo-Christian tradition, which teaches that people are born in sin and must be taught to be righteous, Shinto pays little or no attention to questions of guilt, sorrow, and redemption. Instead, it stresses worldly virtues such as gratitude, sincerity, cooperation, and harmony with other people and with nature. Shinto virtues flow throughout every level of Japanese life, from the home to the workplace, and are the bedrock of the culture.

Shinto Belief

Shinto has no catechism, no sacred book to study, and no written commandments or specific moral code to learn. People are simply expected to try to live in accordance with the will of the kami. Because all Japanese people believe they are distantly descended from the heavenly kami, they also believe that the knowledge of what is right and good can be found within their

own hearts. This does not mean that there will never be trouble in life or that people will never act in ways that cause pain to others, but it is felt that those people are misguided, rather than sinful or evil.

Shinto encourages simplicity and cleanliness as signs of inner goodness. There is a steady emphasis on spiritual and physical purity. Shinto asks its followers to be pure in heart and mind and to be grateful for the many blessings bestowed on them by the kami. How they fulfill those obligations is left to the conscience of the individual. Expectations for living the way of the kami are transmitted by example and through tales and legends, early history, and the norito, or ancient Shinto prayers.

From Shinto mythology, people learn that the kami can act unpredictably and are prone to all-too-human failings such as jealousy, rage, annoyance, vanity, and thoughtlessness. The story of Susanowo and Amaterasu, for example, teaches many lessons. The conflict portrays the deities at their worst— Susanowo betraying his word and causing trouble, Amaterasu sulking in the heavenly cave. But Susanowo's rampage through the heavenly fields is understood as mischievous, not malicious. In the end, he redeems himself by casting the symbols of his troublemaking into the sea and doing good on earth, by using his cleverness to kill the dragon, and by making amends with Amaterasu by giving her the jeweled sword. Uzume, the mirth goddess who brings Amaterasu out of her cave, demonstrates the value of laughter to the world.

The purpose of Shinto worship is to maintain close harmony between people, nature, and the kami. The kami embody the life force and can bring blessings to humans, yet they may act in unpredictable ways, disrupting the natural order, as when Amaterasu darkened the world by withdrawing to the cave. People remind the kami of human presence by continually venerating and thanking them for the beauty and bounty of nature and for health and prosperity.

Shinto followers focus on life on this earth, to which they give the highest value. The kami are the spiritual forces that inspire the world, giving it life and protecting from harm those who live in it.

Individual Worship

In Shinto, individual worship is more important than doctrine or belief, and people learn from birth the habit of gratitude to the kami. There are no regular services as such. Rather, people observe Shinto practices as they feel the need. Some limit their participation to annual festivals; others stop at their local shrine every day or perform simple rites before their kamidana, or home altar. Those rites may consist only of freshening the arrangement of gifts on the altar and pausing for a few seconds to bow with clasped hands.

Before they make a formal visit to a shrine, Shinto worshipers customarily follow simple rituals to prepare themselves for worship. Because cleanliness, which symbolizes purity, is a Shinto virtue, many people bathe and put on clean clothes in anticipation of worship. Worshipers then approach their shrine through the *torii*, or ritual gate. A path runs from the gate to the shrine itself, and along the path is running water in some form—either a natural spring or pond or a fountain—with a stone basin that worshipers use for ritual purification.

Worshipers wash their hands. Then, with a dipper provided for the purpose, they take a little water in their cupped hands—never touching the water source with their lips—and transfer the water to their mouth to swish around or gargle lightly. Only then do they proceed to the shrine.

Shinto worship takes place outside the shrine, not within. To get the attention of the kami within the shrine, the worshiper bows low twice and then rings a shrine bell and claps twice. The kami having been summoned, the worshiper bows again and offers a prayer, either asking for the blessing of the resident kami or thanking them for their goodness.

It is customary but not essential to leave a small offering of money or food, such as a few coins or a few grains of rice wrapped in paper, a rice cake, or a little sake (Japanese rice wine), for the kami. Worshipers may write prayer requests on slips of white paper and attach them to the sacred sakaki tree that is usually nearby. If the shrine is a large one, there may be a booth on the grounds where people may buy prayer or fortune slips, which they may either leave behind or take back to their *kamidana,* or home altar, if they have one. The offerings made to the kami are tokens of appreciation, not sacrifices. Sacrifice is unknown in Shinto. People approach the kami with pure hearts, and they leave satisfied that their prayer has been heard.

Ritual in Shinto Worship

Having no creed or scripture, Shinto relies greatly on ritual to transmit religious thought and feeling. The kami are believed to appreciate and respond to ritual, and correctly performing ritual is an important way to communicate with them.

Apart from those simple rituals performed by individuals, Shinto ritual is conducted by priests who have studied its ancient forms. All ceremonies contain four elements: purification, offering, supplication, and feast.

Purification, or *harai,* removes the pollution, unrighteousness, and evil that keep worshipers from being able to communicate with the kami. The symbolic rinsing of hands and mouth before proceeding to a shrine is a simple purification ritual for individuals. Performed by a priest, it includes a prayer, the waving of a purification wand, and, often, the sprinkling of salt or salt water, which has purifying powers.

Offerings, or *shinshen,* are simple gifts made to the kami on a regular basis, ideally at least once a day. Shinto followers believe that if this duty to the kami is neglected, the kami will be unhappy and will fail to provide their continued support and blessings. In homes and at small shrines, offerings may be a few coins, bits of food, or flowers. At larger shrines, offerings are presented according to the ritual of the shrine, often after priests have purified them. Food and drink—particularly rice and sake, but also water and other food, such as fish and vegetables—are frequent offerings. Other gifts may include silk or cotton cloth, money, jewelry, and perhaps the product of an industry. Sacred dances, sports, and drama, which entertain the kami, are also forms of offering.

The classic prayers, or norito, of Shinto are spoken in ancient Japanese, which modern speakers no longer understand. The prayers were composed in antiquity in rhythmic poetry that was believed to be pleasing to the ear of the kami. A norito must

■ *Led by Shinto priests, visitors to the ancient Togo Shrine walk through a large ring of reeds during the Purification Ceremony. It is believed the unique purification rites will bring good health and luck to its participants.*

be pronounced exactly as it was composed or it loses its effectiveness in reaching the kami. Newer prayers are drafted by the Association of Shrine Shinto for use in its shrines, and prayers may be composed by priests as well. In general, the prayers begin with praise of the kami, refer to the origin of the ritual being performed, offer thanks, make appropriate requests, and end with words of respect for the kami's powers.

All formal Shinto ceremonies end with a symbolic feast, or *naorai,* which means "to eat with the kami." At the close of the ceremony, worshipers are offered a sip of sake or water; during festivals, people may adjourn to enjoy a festive meal.

Origins of the Shinto Priesthood

Originally, the priestly duties of Shinto were carried out by clan leaders. But as the clans combined and recombined into larger and larger units, several families began to dominate, and a priestly class emerged. The priesthood became hereditary. The priestly families traced their ancestry back to the kami who accompanied Ninigi from the high plains of heaven on his mission to rule the earth.

The early imperial court granted authority to four families. One was in charge of rituals and ceremonies. A second was charged with remaining ritually pure and keeping in constant contact with the kami. A third was responsible for learning the will of the kami, and the members of the fourth family were the dancers and musicians. A few ceremonies were performed by the emperor alone, but for the most part, those four families were in charge of all Shinto rites. Shinto priests were not required to be celibate as are Catholic priests, for example. Prayers and rituals were passed down from father to son, generation to generation.

The establishment of State Shinto changed the makeup of the priesthood. Hereditary positions were abolished, and priests were appointed by the government. In practice, many of the priests under the hereditary system were reappointed by local officials, but at important shrines in the cities, the positions were given to well-connected people of high social standing.

The Modern Priesthood

Today, Shinto priests are private citizens. Except for those who administer large shrines, many work at other jobs. They can be teachers, office workers, or businesspeople. They marry and

■ *Shinto priests make offerings at the height of a Shinto ceremony. The Shinto priest on the left is celebrating the Fall Festival at the Hiro-Hachiman Shrine in Hiragawa. He is helped by visiting Shinto priests and his daughter. The priest at this shrine is also a social studies teacher at a local school.*

live with their families, occasionally in houses on shrine grounds but often in the community. Unless they are conducting ritual at a shrine, they dress in ordinary street clothes.

The priest's job is to know Shinto ritual and liturgy and how to conduct Shinto festivals and ceremonies. People study to be priests either privately with another priest, by attending classes sponsored by the Association of Shrine Shinto, or by taking courses at a seminary or university. Trained candidates are appointed by the Association of Shrine Shinto.

Before a festival, the priests who will conduct the ceremony seclude themselves from other people to prepare themselves spiritually. They bathe, put on clean clothes, eat only certain foods, and concentrate on leading a calm and controlled life. Any violation of the rules of abstinence disqualifies them from participating in the ceremonies.

Women Priests

Although Shinto priesthood was traditionally male, there has never been a rule against women priests. At those times when the ruler of Japan was an empress, the role of head priest passed to her. The shrine to Amaterasu at Ise, considered the most sacred of all Shinto shrines, traditionally has a high priestess, usually a member of the imperial family, in addition to a high priest. During World War II, when most Japanese men were engaged in the war effort, their wives and daughters took over priestly duties. Many women proved to be able administrators of large shrines. After the war, the newly formed Association of Shrine Shinto recognized the women's service to the Shinto religion and welcomed their participation.

Shrine Maidens

In addition to a staff of priests, many larger shrines also have *miko*, or shrine maidens, who participate in Shinto ceremonies. Miko are young, unmarried women, the daughters of priests or local shrine members, who learn the sacred dances and perform them as a part of Shinto ritual. The miko wear a traditional costume of white kimono and red divided skirt. In addition to ceremonial dance, miko may perform other parts of the

A shrine maiden strikes the gong at the Meiji-Jingu Shrine, Tokyo, Japan.

ritual, such as distributing the symbolic feast to the people after the ceremony or selling talismans and charms on shrine grounds. Like other celebrants of Shinto, they otherwise lead ordinary lives, attending school and living in the community. When they marry, other girls and young women take their place.

The Shinto Ceremony

Before a Shinto ceremony, the priests and musicians gather, along with the local dignitaries and their representatives who will also participate. They go in procession to the place of purification. After purification, they proceed to the inner sanctuary of the shrine. All bow deeply. As music plays and the other participants remain in a position of deep reverence, the chief priest opens the doors of the inner sanctuary. He chants a special "*ooo-ing*" sound that attracts the kami. The priests then make offerings of food and any other gifts. After each offering, there is a prayer, and a priest or other specially trained person performs a sacred dance.

The worshipers then go one by one to make a symbolic offering, usually a sprig of the sacred sakaki tree, placing it on a special stand, clapping and bowing in the traditional Shinto way. In a large festival, one representative is chosen to make the offering for all, who clap and bow in unison. After all offerings have been made, the worshipers bow deeply again, and the priest removes the offerings and closes the door to the sanctuary, again with special chanting. The priests and other participants withdraw to partake of the symbolic feast. The worshipers receive a sip of wine or water. Food offerings may later be shared with the members of the shrine.

Purification Ritual

A typical purification ritual is *yutate*, or immersion in hot water. The priests heat two caldrons of water over a fire. When the water is hot, they put out the fire. Then the head priest takes a branch of the sacred sakaki tree to which strips of white paper, symbolizing the kami, are attached, and waves it over the head of the other priests, the shrine maidens, and the officials and patrons of the shrine, usually local businesspeople. The priest speaks a norito. Then the shrine maidens do a sacred dance. Finally, one maiden, dressed in white, tosses salt onto the ground around the cauldrons to purify it and adds small amounts of rice and sake to the cauldrons in a ritual manner. She then takes a wooden bowl and scoop and, from the air above, scoops nectar of the kami and pours it into the cauldrons. Next, she fills the bowl from a cauldron and gives it to a priest, who carries it into the shrine to the altar, thus making it sacred.

The shrine maiden then stirs the sacred water with leafy bamboo branches and waves the branches over the people, sprinkling them lightly with drops of warm water as she speaks special words. The water from the cauldrons is then passed around for all to drink, uniting them with the kami.

The purification ritual incorporates the basic Shinto values of purification, renewal, gratitude, and respect for the kami. It also shares the powers of the kami with the people and creates a heightened sense of community and cooperation. As always, its aim is to maintain a harmonious relationship between the kami and the people.

The Importance of Worship

Regular individual worship and proper ritual are vital parts of Shinto. Through these forms, people express their gratitude to the kami, the life force behind all things in creation. This expression of gratitude maintains the balance between humans, the natural world, and kami. The relationship is reciprocal; having been thanked and revered, the kami return the favor by continuing to provide blessings to the people. Thus worship of the kami gives people access to their life-giving powers.

CHAPTER 7

The Shinto Year: Festivals and Rites of Passage

S hinto is a religion of festivals and rejoicing. Each shrine has its own yearly calendar of rituals and festivals, and each calendar can vary from shrine to shrine. The festivals of the Shinto calendar often overlap with the religious holidays of other traditions, and all are part of the annual events, or *nenju gyoji*, of Japan. These include both religious festivals and regional and national celebrations. Although today many Shinto festivals, or matsuri, seem more secular than religious, most began as religious celebrations, and the word *matsuri* connotes prayer and worship along with festival and fun.

Shinto began in a farming society, and its festivals follow the agrarian calendar. Spring festivals mark the time of rice planting, a critical time in rice culture. In the fall there are festivals to commemorate harvest and thanksgiving. The new year is celebrated as a time of purification and renewal and is very important because it symbolizes a new start. But festivals also celebrate smaller wonders: cherry blossoms in the spring, the blooms of summer, and the changing of leaves in the fall. Occupations have guardian deities, and yearly festivals are held to thank them for their protection. In addition, apart from the yearly activities that occur at all Shinto shrines, each shrine celebrates a festival for its own particular guardian deity or deities.

Shinto Festivals

Festivals are, first of all, times to enjoy. When festival days arrive, businesses and factories shut down, and families and neighbors get together, frequently on the spacious grounds surrounding a shrine. The larger shrines often have outbuildings in which people can gather for entertainment. Actors may present *Noh*, classic dance-dramas that depict stories of the kami, plays about early Shinto history, or comedies, because the kami love to laugh. Shrine maidens perform dances to entertain the kami. Merchants set up stalls on shrine grounds to sell snacks, drinks, toys, and games.

Festivals may last one day or as long as a week. They may include jugglers, wrestlers, horse races, archery, bonfires, boat races; some of the larger festivals involve the entire population, even in major cities like Kyoto.

Within every shrine is a shintai—a sacred object symbolizing the essence of the kami to whom the shrine is dedicated. This sacred object is wrapped in silk and enclosed in a box that is never opened. The shintai is never seen, even by the priests, and worshipers take its existence on faith. At festival time, priests place this box in a *mikoshi*, or palanquin, a decorated chest carried by means of long, horizontal poles. Strong young men carry this palanquin around the town so the kami can see the locale over which they preside and bless it or simply enjoy it. The men make sure that the mikoshi passes each house in the town so that the relationship between the kami and the people is reinforced. Important, too, is the fact that the very act of carrying the mikoshi requires close cooperation among the men. A small palanquin may require four to eight bearers; some of the larger ones may require thirty. The shared task reminds the men of their dependence on one another, a traditional Shinto virtue.

At larger festivals, processions may also include huge wheeled floats, sometimes two stories high, colorfully decorated, and pulled by young men. The floats may present historical scenes or may carry dancers and musicians who perform for the crowds. People join the processions dressed in historical costumes—traditional kimonos and court dress or the regalia of ancient warriors.

■ *The Gion Matsuri, an annual festival held on July 17 in Kyoto, features a parade with huge floats that carry musicians and other performers. The festival attracts visitors from all over the world.*

Shinto ritual, of course, is an important part of the festival. Priests perform ancient rituals of purification, offering, supplication, and feast. Colorfully dressed shrine maidens dance for the entertainment of the kami. Prayers ask for a continuation of the blessings of the kami. Throughout the festival, worshipers approach the shrine, ring the shrine bell, clap, and present their own offerings and prayers to the kami.

The New Year's Festival

The New Year's Festival, which lasts for seven days, is the country's most important Shinto celebration. It is both a national holiday and a religious event—a time to celebrate, pay debts, make amends, and begin anew. During this festival, people dress in kimonos, traditional Japanese dress, and women do up their hair in traditional styles. The streets are festooned with banners and other colorful decorations.

Before the New Year's Festival begins, people clean their homes, symbolically sweeping out the old year, with its bad luck and sorrow, and making room for the new. About the house they hang pine branches, which symbolize renewal of life, and rice-straw ropes, which define sacred space and ward off evil. It is also customary to put pine boughs in bamboo baskets because in Japan bamboo is a symbol of strength and growth. Some people set up a special altar in their homes to welcome ancestors and rice kami, who return in January.

For a Shinto family, one of the first acts of the new year is to visit the local shrine. Beginning at midnight, worshipers approach the shrine to pay respects and to ask the kami for help in the coming year. Outside the shrine may be hung a rice-straw rope through which the people pass before they enter the shrine precincts, symbolically leaving their impurities behind, so they may be fresh and pure when they meet the kami. Inside, they toss coins into a box as a symbolic offering, then offer their prayers. Often they make resolutions for the new year and request assistance in keeping them. This visit to the shrine is an act of purification, the shedding of old impurities and the beginning of a new life.

At the shrine they may buy new charms to place on their altar. A popular charm takes the shape of an arrow, a Shinto symbol that carries the meaning of destroying evil. They may purchase *ema*, wooden votive tablets on which their requests may be written. They may also buy fortune slips on white paper, which they read and then tie to temple trees. In this way, the whole community shares any good luck included in the fortune, while any bad luck may blow away.

The New Year's Festival includes the formal Shinto ritual in which priests chant norito. Shrine maidens, the young girls whose families are members of the shrine, wear traditional costumes and dance *kagura*, or sacred dances, to entertain the kami. Shrine maidens also participate in some of the rituals and help in the business of the shrine, selling talismans and giving bless-

■ **Rice Culture**

Rice, the food that has sustained the Japanese since prehistory, is planted by broadcasting the grains freely in a small field and flooding the area with water. Three or four weeks later, the young seedlings are transplanted into carefully spaced rows about 18 inches apart in a larger walled field, which is then also flooded. Transplanting is a critical stage in rice culture; if the grain fails to sprout, it can be replanted, but if transplantation fails, the crop is lost. Shinto festivals to ensure the success of the rice crop are therefore held, not at planting time, but at the time the rice is transplanted.

ings. New Year's Festival rites help people begin the new year pure in heart and in contact with kami.

■ *In Tokyo, a typical wrestler prepares for a sumo match by engaging in a Shinto ritual to drive evil spirits away from the ring.*

During these festivities, it is customary for businesses and other organizations to make substantial gifts to the local shrine, thanking the kami for their support in the past and asking for success in the future. Gifts may be related to the contributor's business but are more commonly food and sake. Sake is a popular gift. After it has been consecrated, it is shared by the worshipers, adding to the festival atmosphere.

On the first night of the new year, people may celebrate all night. At the smaller countryside shrines, worshipers drift away by one o'clock in the morning. But many leave to board trains that run through the night to nearby national shrines. Major shrines, such as the Meiji Shrine in Tokyo and Fushimi Inari in Kyoto, boast huge crowds of more than a million people on New Year's night.

After the first night, the celebration becomes quieter, but people continue to gather in a holiday mood. Extended families get together at this time, and spirits of ancestors are believed to visit as well, so the celebrations include both living members and ancestor spirits. They give *oseibo*, or year-end gifts, a custom adopted from Europe and America.

The old charms or talismans, bought during the past year and left at the local shrine during the New Year's Festival, become part of the next Shinto ceremony. On January 15, or Little New Year's, priests ritually destroy the old charms by burning them while chanting ancient Shinto prayers. The fire eradicates the bad luck absorbed by the charms over the year, reinforcing the renewal of the new year. This ritual also welcomes the rice kami back for another year of prosperity.

The Great Purification

Purification is an essential part of all Shinto worship, and the New Year's Festival includes the Shinto rite known as the Great Purification. This rite removes the impurities people have accumulated since the last purification ritual.

The Great Purification ritual symbolically recreates Izanagi's act of bathing when he returned from his trip to Yomi, the underworld. As he purified himself, he brought forth new kami, including Susanowo and Amaterasu. Thus, purification has power over death, and living people may return to a state of purity. Purification brings people closer to the kami.

The Great Purification takes place at all local shrines twice a year, during the New Year's Festival and at the end of June or the beginning of July. A priest recites the *Oharai*, or Great Purification norito, and then waves a purification wand in a ritual pattern before the assembled worshipers. The Oharai is a song in praise of life, spoken in the ancient Yamato language from which modern Japanese comes. Shinto followers believe that each word has its own soul, and when the words of a norito are chanted together as they have been chanted since the time of the kami, they unite people with the kami. Listeners are exhorted to feel the rhythm and spirit of the prayer, which is directed at washing away impurities in themselves and in the nation as a whole.

During the Great Purification, people may rub a human figure cut from paper over their bodies, symbolically rubbing away impurity. The paper, like the talismans at a New Year's Festival, is later ritually destroyed by the priests, ridding the people of anything impure.

Nenju Gyoji: The National Events

In Japan, there are national holidays or major festivals almost every month, featuring parades, parties, games, and a time to dress up in traditional clothes. The New Year's Festival is the biggest, but there are many other occasions for celebration.

February 3 is celebrated as the last day of winter and the beginning of spring. People throw soybeans out of the house and symbolically drive out evil and impurity. Children gather soybeans that are tossed out of the shrines and bring them home for luck. On a day close to the spring equinox, around March 21, local shrines conduct a spring festival during which people visit the shrines to make offerings to the kami, a reminder of the seasonal rhythms and the links between humans, the kami, and nature. Early April brings a flower festival. This was traditionally the time when the mountain kami came down from the hills and entered the rice fields to be rice kami for the rest of the season. In celebration, people climbed the mountains and carried down armloads of flowers, signifying the coming of spring and the bounty of nature. Today, people picnic and hike in the mountains to celebrate the festival.

After the Great Purification comes the Festival of the Dead in July. Originally a Buddhist festival, this event is now commemorated by all. Homes are cleaned and ancestors are welcomed with special offerings. Families visit cemeteries and decorate memorial stones with flowers.

Close to the fall equinox in mid-September is a fall festival, a kind of Thanksgiving that marks the return of the rice kami to the mountains for another year and thanks them for the rice harvest. People again visit graves to honor ancestors and receive their blessing. In December comes the preparation for the New Year's Festival, and the ritual year begins again.

Rites of Passage

Shinto, like all religions, marks times in human life: birth, marriage, and death. It places great emphasis on beginnings, fertility, and growth, so birth and childhood are much celebrated in Shinto families with special events for children.

Miyamairi

At birth, a child receives its soul from its birth kami, the guardian of the place where it was born. When the baby is one month old and free from the impurities associated with birth, its parents take it to their local shrine for *miyamairi*, a birth ritual. At that time, the baby becomes *ujiko*, a parishioner of that shrine, and comes under the protection of the shrine's guardian kami. Traditionally, this is the baby's first trip outside its home. By taking it to the shrine, its parents accept for it the responsibility of supporting the shrine and participating in festivals and Shinto ritual. The birth ritual affirms that the kami are the source of the child's life and establishes a relationship between the child and the kami.

Boys' and Girls' Festivals

Many other celebrations with Shinto roots mark the life of a child. Boys and girls have their own festivals. Girls may participate in the Doll Festival, which takes place on March 3. During this festival, girls arrange displays of intricately carved dolls,

 Young participants gather to celebrate Shichigosan, a day of prayer for children.

many of which have been handed down through generations, and invite friends and neighbors for tea. At one time, this was a time of purification, when people made paper figures to which they transferred their impurities and threw them into the sea.

A Boy's Festival takes place on May 5. Soldier dolls placed outside the entry to the house symbolically drive away evil. Boys arrange displays of miniature samurai, signifying strength and courage, and hang wind-socks that depict the carp, the symbol of strength and vitality. These boy-and-girl festivals, which are now celebrated more as times of family get-togethers than as religious holidays, have lost most of their religious significance, but they still serve to remind children of the nearness of the kami to their lives.

Shichigosan

The annual Shichigosan, or seven–five–three, is a day of prayer for the welfare of children. Widely celebrated, it takes place in November. Girls of three and seven and boys of five are dressed in their best clothes or in traditional costumes and taken for a visit to their tutelary shrine. There they pray to the kami to protect them and help them to grow and be pure and strong.

Coming of Age

Coming-of-age rites have disappeared from Shinto worship, although January 15 is celebrated across Japan as an official coming of age for all those who reach the age of twenty that year and thus can marry without parental consent. In the countryside, a young man's coming to maturity is marked by inviting him to help carry the palanquin in a festival parade.

Marriage Before Kami

One widely observed celebration is the Shinto wedding. In the past, Shinto weddings were conducted at home, but today Shinto shrines with beautiful grounds are popular places for "marriage before kami," and many Japanese couples choose a Shinto ceremony. Marriage in Japan has always been viewed as a contract between two families, so it is not conducted by a priest but by the couple themselves.

In Japan, October is the month for weddings. The bride may wear a modern Western-style wedding dress, or she may choose traditional Japanese wedding clothes: a special kimono and a tall wig with long hairpins and a wide white headband. According to custom, the headdress hides the "horns" of female jealousy. Traditional garb for the groom was a kimono and divided pants, but today most grooms choose to wear a Western-style suit or a tuxedo. As a pledge of their union, the couple sip rice wine from three cups. Their families then sip the wine to show loyalty to the new family that is being formed. A wedding feast follows the ceremony.

Funerals

Old Shinto did not have funeral rites, which came into the religion from Buddhism. Most Japanese are still "born Shinto, die Buddhist," choosing Buddhist ceremonies for funerals. But Shinto priests may conduct solemn prayers for the dead at Shinto shrines as well. The funeral ceremony marks the beginning of the dead person's new life as an ancestor who, having lived life to the fullest in accordance with the will of the kami, will continue to bring prosperity and blessings to the living.

The Shinto Calendar in Japanese Life

Shinto festivals have different focuses. Some aim at ensuring the well-being of particular communities by appealing for assistance from their kami and the souls of their ancestors. The goals of such celebrations are to attain fruitful harvests, to escape crop damage, or to avoid natural disasters. Purification rites are meant to cleanse the participants from the pollutions that separate them from the kami and the revered dead. Ritual prayers seek a favorable response from gods and ancestors. Other festivals are more active, including various contests on horses or in boats, ceremonial dances, and taxing processions. The latter are meant to increase the vitality of the kami and the participants as the time of planting or harvesting is at hand. Such celebrations might be religious for some, but for others they are just rituals of modern society. The snow festival held at Sapporo is a secular celebration that aims mainly at drawing tourists to the area.

Festivals such as the Doll's Festival (Hinu Matsuri) on March 3 or the Boy's Festival (Tango no Sekku) on May 5 are not tied to the land and its fruits, but rather are celebrations centered in family life in concert with friends and neighbors.

Other festivals go beyond the borders of farm communities or families in their aims. The New Year's Festival is a national and religious holiday. It is viewed as a time to pay debts, make apologies, and turn a new leaf.

No matter the number of the participants, all these efforts bind the people together. Shinto celebrations throughout the year help unite people as families, as farm or city communities, and as a nation.

CHAPTER 8

Sacred Places and Spaces

*J*apan, a country about the size of the state of California in the United States, has more than 80,000 Shinto shrines. Some are elaborate buildings patterned after Buddhist temples, with lanterns, statues, and paintings. Others are small, simple structures in peaceful natural settings or along the roadside. Still others are not buildings at all, but natural objects marked with a rice-straw rope to signify sacred space.

The Sacred Land

In early times, people worshiped in nature. They climbed mountains to catch the first glimpse of Amaterasu, the rising sun, at dawn, and they went to ocean shores near where the sea kami controlled the tides and the fish that fed the village. They found evidence of kami presence in great rocks and enormous trees, in deep valleys and beside rushing water, and they worshiped beside them. Those traditions still remain.

Every town and locality has its own shrine housing its guardian kami. Many towns also have shrines that commemorate special people or events. Shinto shrines belong to everyone

and are everyone's responsibility. Even in rural areas, at shrines that stand deep in wooded areas, many miles from towns or cities, and even where there are no regular priests, it is rare to find shrine grounds that are not carefully tended. The shrines and the grounds on which they are situated are all sacred land, treated with reverence.

Cities, too, have sacred associations. Kyoto and Nara, former Japanese capitals, are sacred cities because their history is entwined with that of the imperial line. These cities have many shrines that date back to ancient times and are designated national treasures.

In a larger sense, however, all of Japan is sacred ground. It was formed by the kami for the Japanese people, and everything in it is inhabited by kami. Kami dwell in all its geographical features, its mountains, trees, and flowers, the sea and the rivers, and even the highways and roads. There is no part of Japan that the kami do not touch, for kami can be anywhere and are everywhere. All of the land therefore demands, and receives, great respect from its inhabitants.

The Japanese are a nation of people who love to visit the beautiful places in their own country. As "tourists," they often plan their vacations around visits to sacred waterfalls or mountains, which symbolize the presence of kami everywhere. To climb Mount Fuji is not merely to go sightseeing but to be in the presence of the sacred, and many Japanese tours include an element of pilgrimage.

The Shinto Home

According to Shinto tradition, the home itself is blessed by the kami and therefore sacred. It is the center of Shinto religious life. Ritual is performed within it, and kami reside there. Family worship within the home is central to the Shinto tradition.

Shinto ritual accompanies the building of a house. Special ceremonies consecrate the homesite and accompany various stages of the actual building, such as laying the foundation or raising the roof. There are kami in every part of the house: threshold kami, kitchen kami, fireplace kami, even toilet kami, who keep away impurity and disease.

The Kamidana

At one time, every Japanese house had a kamidana, or kami-shelf, enshrining kami in the home. This small altar contained a replica of a Shinto-style shrine. Each day, household members made prayers and offerings at the kamidana as they would at a shrine, by bowing and clapping to summon ancestors and the guardian kami of their home and offering thanks. They kept the offerings on the kamidana fresh, replenishing foodstuffs, such as a rice cake or a little sake, morning and night, or adding fresh flowers. On the kamidana, also, went talismans and charms bought at the local shrine or at one of the national shrines during a trip or pilgrimage, bringing the blessings of those kami to the home as well. During the time when Buddhist altars were mandatory in Japanese homes, kamidana remained, often side by side with the Buddhist altar, and people paid their respects to the deities at both altars. Many modern Japanese homes no longer have kamidana, although traditional households still follow the custom.

Local Shrines

Shinto began as a local religion, and every locality has its own shrine, with its own tutelary, or guardian, kami. By custom, people come under the protection of the guardian kami of the place where they were born, and they remain under that kami's protection all their lives. Annual religious events, such as the New Year's Festival or the Great Purification, are held at the local shrine, as are local festivals. People go individually to their shrine to give thanks to the kami for blessings in their own lives and in the community as a whole.

Besides being a place for ritual, festival, and private worship, the grounds of the local shrine serve as a community center in which meetings and recreational activities are held. People use shrine precincts as they would a park, for picnics and games, or just to sit and enjoy the pleasant surroundings.

Beyond the locality, there may be area shrines honoring other kami. A seaside village, for example, might have both a shrine to its tutelary deities and a shrine to the kami of fishers or the kami of sailors.

During annual festivals, families traditionally visit their local shrine and participate in the rituals that bring them into closer contact with their tutelary kami. At the shrines people can buy talismans and charms to take back to their homes, thus ensuring the presence there of the guardian kami. So the protection of the local kami is transferred to the home, completing the circle of sacredness.

Shrine Structure

At its simplest, a Shinto shrine is a rectangular space to which the kami come. A traditional shrine is made of natural materials, such as rough-hewn timber, unpainted wood, thatch, and stone. Shrines are not large. Priests enter them to perform rites, but people stand outside to worship. Inside the shrine is an

A Shinto priest performs a rite before the offering table in the Meiji Shrine in Tokyo, Japan.

altar or an inner sanctuary, tended by Shinto priests, containing a silk-lined box that holds an object that symbolizes the heavenly kami, encased in a silk-lined box.

The interior of a shrine has no decoration. There are no representations of kami within a shrine, neither pictures nor statues. There may be a display of ordinary objects, such as stones, swords or bow and arrows, beads, and perhaps a mirror, any of which might be sacred to the various kami, but images of them are unnecessary because the kami themselves are there.

Small shrines often stand alone, but larger shrines may be part of a complex containing a number of sanctuaries and auxiliary buildings. A large shrine compound may have an oratory, or

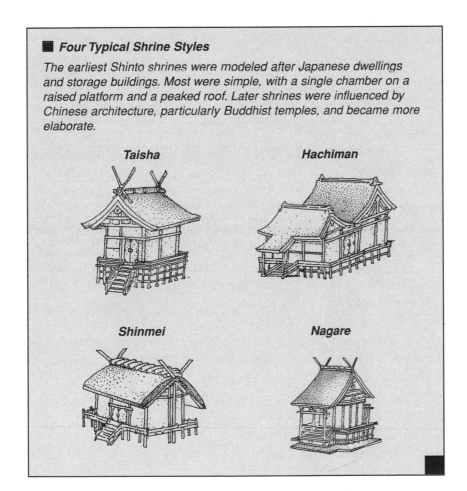

■ *Four Typical Shrine Styles*

The earliest Shinto shrines were modeled after Japanese dwellings and storage buildings. Most were simple, with a single chamber on a raised platform and a peaked roof. Later shrines were influenced by Chinese architecture, particularly Buddhist temples, and became more elaborate.

Taisha

Hachiman

Shinmei

Nagare

speaker's stand, a pavilion with flowing water for ritual purification, a building in which to prepare food offerings, a shrine office, an auditorium for sacred dances, and a pavilion where people may leave votive tablets or other offerings, along with one or more sanctuaries and other structures.

Whenever possible, shrines are placed near water, and many shrine grounds still contain a spring, a brook, or a pond. In ancient times, worshipers dipped up a little water from a stream or the sea to rinse their hands and mouths. Today, every shrine approach has an ablution pavilion, a place where people may stop to purify themselves ritually before they worship. Often this pavilion is an open shed with a stone basin and running water.

Many shrines include stalls or a small shop from which people can get charms and talismans for their kamidana, or home altar, in return for a small offering. Throughout the year, these are sold to pilgrims and visitors at festivals and at the larger shrines with national significance.

The Shrine Grounds

Shrine grounds are themselves sacred land. Over centuries, many shrines have been carefully sited in places that evoke feelings of respect and awe because of their natural beauty, perhaps near a mountain, a grove of trees, a river, or overlooking the ocean. Others are located where some historical event took place or where an ancient and respected family lived.

Much effort goes into making the shrine grounds a place of peaceful beauty. Even in cities, where land is scarce and grounds may be small, trees and plantings evoke a natural setting and suggest the closeness of nature.

Shrines usually face south or sometimes east; north and west are considered unlucky directions. Customarily, a fence or a wall surrounds the shrine grounds, and there may be inner fences as well, perhaps enclosed by a gate.

Torii, the Symbol of Shinto

Worshipers enter the shrine through a torii, a gateway that symbolizes the separation of the outside world from the world of the kami and marks the entrance into sacred space. There are many styles of torii, but each is distinctive in basic design. Originally, the torii consisted of two unfinished wooden pillars with two crossbeams. Later, under outside architectural influences, the pillars were planed smooth and painted, usually red, and eventually came to be made of other materials, such as metal or concrete.

A large shrine may have a row of torii through which worshipers pass. The Fushimi Inari Shrine in Tokyo has more than ten thousand scarlet-painted torii, in a line almost two and a half miles (four kilometers) long.

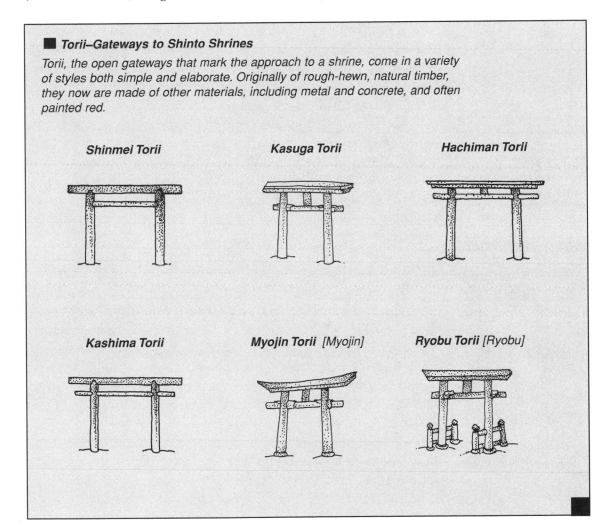

■ Torii–Gateways to Shinto Shrines

Torii, the open gateways that mark the approach to a shrine, come in a variety of styles both simple and elaborate. Originally of rough-hewn, natural timber, they now are made of other materials, including metal and concrete, and often painted red.

Shinmei Torii

Kasuga Torii

Hachiman Torii

Kashima Torii

Myojin Torii [Myojin]

Ryobu Torii [Ryobu]

The Approach

Worshipers pass through the torii on a path that leads to the shrine. This is the *sando*, or approach. It is usually a dirt path spread with pebbles or neatly raked packed sand, and it contributes to the natural atmosphere. Ideally, the path winds through the grounds, but if the area is small, it may go directly to the shrine.

Lanterns made of stone or bronze, donated by worshipers, often line the approach. Elaborate lanterns are a borrowing from Buddhism, but fire, a purifying element in Shinto ritual, has always been a traditional means of greeting the kami. Along the path, too, may be stone tablets memorializing local national historic events. There may also be a stone pillar called a *hykudo ishi*, or hundred times stone. Worshipers with a particularly urgent request may walk back and forth one hundred times between the stone and the shrine to emphasize their plea.

Since many shrines are in natural settings, the grounds may contain ancient trees or great rocks that traditionally have kami presence. If so, these often have a rice-straw rope around them to show their special sacredness. Almost every shrine has on its grounds a sakaki tree, the sacred tree of Shinto, the tree that the kami hung with jewels and cloth and the mirror to lure Amaterasu out of her cave.

Shrine Guardians

Beside the shrine entrance may be guardians of the shrine precincts. Sometimes these take the form of miniature shrines. At large shrines, the guardians may be huge semi-human figures with angry expressions to ward off evil. These figures were originally Buddhist, but they came to be guardians of Shinto shrines as well. Another traditional guardian pair are two seated figures, each dressed in ancient court garb and each carrying a bow and arrows. They represent mythological kami.

Animal protectors also appear. The most common are male and female lions or dogs, which stand on pedestals along the approach. At Inari shrines, the image is a fox, which is believed to be an attendant of Inari, the rice kami. At Kasuga shrines, the animal guardian is a deer. Other animal images include horses,

■ *Below and on following page-*
Two lions stand guard at the approach to a shrine. At Shinto shrines, animal images in male and female pairs, are symbolic of protection. They usually stand on either side of the torii or along the approach to the shrine.

the traditional mount of the kami, or monkeys and wolves. Like other statuary on Shinto grounds, these shrine guardians reflect Buddhist influence.

Shrine Construction

The earliest Shinto shrines were built like the homes of the Japanese people of the day. They were unadorned square or rectangular structures placed on a platform with a low railing and a stairway to the door. Most were one-room buildings with an inner chamber to hold a sacred symbol of the kami and a place for offerings, either outside or just inside the building. Traditional shrines were made of unpainted, rough-hewn wood, usually cypress, thatched with bark. The buildings themselves were much less impressive than their surroundings and, in their simplicity and naturalness, they were designed to merge with the surrounding area.

Many Shinto shrines have a characteristic roof style. The end beams, or *chigi*, form an X, crossing at the ridge and continuing upward. The ridgepole lies across them, cradled by the crossed beams. On top of the ridgepole are short beams, or *katsuogi*. Originally, they held down the roof, although with modern construction methods they are now purely decorative. The distinctive roof design of a Shinto shrine, however, carries no religious significance. It is simply an antique design that has been carried over into modern times.

As Buddhism gained in popularity and eclipsed Shinto, Buddhist temples and Shinto shrines became more similar in design. Under the influence of Buddhism, shrines became more elaborate and colorful. Shrine interiors were divided into rooms, sometimes under separate roof beams. Later shrines were often painted, most of them red.

Every twenty years, a shrine was taken down and rebuilt in a ceremony of shrine renewal. At that time, the shrine's divine treasures were renewed as well, and the old ones were buried on the shrine grounds. Shrine renewal, which continues today, is more than just refurbishment of old shrines. The accompanying Shinto ritual refreshes and renews the spiritual life of the kami in that place:

Within the Shrine

Within the shrine sanctuary is an inner chamber with two swinging doors that are kept locked except when a priest is performing sacred rites. Inside, on a raised platform or altar, lies the shintai, the sacred object or divine embodiment of the kami enshrined there. The divine object is wrapped in silk and enclosed in a box, which is never opened. A curtain, usually made of split bamboo, hides the box from view, even by the priest. Not all shrines have shintai. Some have *mitamashiro*, or substitute divine treasures, which are usually representations of shintai, such as mirrors or swords. To the Shinto worshiper, it does not matter whether the sacred object is shintai or mitamashiro. The presence of the object sanctifies the building and makes it a home of the kami. If the object is removed, the building is no longer sacred.

In front of the inner chamber is a table for offerings. On or behind the offering table is a *gohei*, a wand hung with paper folded and placed in a ritual manner. The gohei symbolizes the presence of kami and is also a symbolic offering to the kami.

A purification wand with long strips of white paper and flax attached at one end stands nearby. During a ceremony, the priest removes it from its stand and waves it over the person or object to be purified. A branch of the sacred sakaki tree is sometimes used in place of or in addition to the purification wand, and if so, it also rests on the offering table.

Other Shrine Objects

The *Kojiki* tells that Izanagi, one of the creators of Japan, gave his children a polished disk of silver and told them to look at themselves in it to be sure that it reflected only a pure spirit. Many shrines contain mirrors as sacred objects, but in addition, mirrors are often placed before the doors of the inner compartment of a sanctuary as ornaments. Banners may be hung nearby, an ornamental borrowing from Buddhism, now signifying the presence of kami. A sword and shield and jewels are often hung with the banners as symbols of the power of the kami to protect and bless the people, and of the will of the people to defend the kami. Shinto believers understand that the mirror symbolizes

---

■ *The Mirror*

The mirror hides nothing. It shines without a selfish mind. Everything good and bad, right and wrong, is reflected without fail. The mirror is the source of honesty because it has the virtue of responding according to the shape of objects. It points out the fairness and impartiality of the divine will.

from *Jinno Shotoki*, by Chikafusa Kitabatake (1339).

---

wisdom, the jewels, a giving and benevolent spirit, and the sword, courage.

Beginning around the seventh century C.E., shrine buildings also housed divine treasures for use by the kami, who were deemed to be always within. Daggers, swords, archery equipment, furniture, clothing, jewelry, and musical instruments were made by master craftspeople and displayed. Shinto artists produced paintings and sculpture for the honor of the kami as well. Many works of sculpture were monumental or life-size images of kami carved from single tree trunks, thus preserving their kami nature. They, too, went to the shrines, where they were placed behind a screen or curtain so as not to distract the worshiper.

The Shrine at Ise

The shrine of Amaterasu at Ise is the most revered of all Shinto shrines. Amaterasu, the tutelary deity of the imperial line, is worshiped there at the inner shrine, Naiku, as the symbol of the Japanese state. The Ise Shrine compound also contains a second major shrine, the outer shrine, Geku, to the harvest kami, about four miles away.

The shrine grounds at Ise are large and ancient. Three torii mark the entrance to the shrines. Huge cedars, *Cryptomeria japonica*, some more than 50 feet tall and densely planted, line the way. The Isuzu River runs through the grounds, and the winding gravel approach takes worshipers close to the water so they may use it to cleanse their hands and mouths according to ancient custom. The crunching of gravel underfoot discourages talk, so people move mostly in silence along the approach, feeling the presence of the divine. Worshipers customarily do not take requests to Ise but go in purity of heart and mind to hear the will of the kami.

The main shrine buildings, in pure classical Shinmei style and surrounded by raked white stones, sit behind four high fences, or curtains. They are simple rectangles, about 47 by 30 feet (15 by 9 meters) and rising about 35 feet (12 meters). The thatched roofs are about 3 feet (1 meter) thick, topped by katsuogi—ten on the shrine to Amaterasu, nine on the Naiku

Shrine. The shrine at Ise dates to 685 and the reign of Emperor Temmu. By his order, its design cannot be used or copied in other buildings, so it is unique.

The buildings at the shrine at Ise are renewed every twenty years, also by order of Emperor Temmu. They have been rebuilt more than sixty times, always in exact replica. The bridges and walkways that link the buildings are renewed as well, in a continuous program of rebuilding. The teams of carpenters who maintain the shrine wear white, the color of purity, and ritually purify themselves as they work. If so much as one drop of blood falls on a piece of wood, it is discarded so that ritual purity may be maintained in the building.

The Naiku Shrine has a long association with the imperial family. Only high-ranking priests and priestesses and members of the imperial family or their representatives enter the shrine. By custom, the emperor visits Ise at the times of important national festivals and other national events to inform Amaterasu personally. In modern times, Emperor Hirohito as a young man went to the shrine before traveling out of the country, on the occasion of his wedding, and at his coronation. During World War II, he kept Amaterasu apprised of the course of the war, and after Japan's defeat, he returned to Ise to explain and apologize for what had happened. Important national events are announced at Ise. When the crown prince was married, he and his bride went first to Ise.

The sacred object at the Naiku Shrine is the mirror given by Amaterasu to her great-grandson Ninigi when she sent him to rule earth, telling him to worship it as her spirit. Originally it was handed down within the imperial family and kept at the palace shrine, but because of its great significance to the nation and the Japanese people, it was moved to the grand shrine at Ise. The imperial shrine now has a replica. The imperial family retains Amaterasu's jewels. The third piece of imperial regalia, the sword of Susanowo, is kept at the Atsuta Shrine in Nagoya.

Ise attracts many visitors each year. Families, schoolchildren, young and old people, businesspeople and workers, all travel to Ise to enjoy its beauty and to be spiritually refreshed by its sacredness. The shrine at Ise is one of Japan's great national

■ *Following page-The shrine buildings at Ise, sacred to Amaterasu, are in the Shinmei, or "divine brightness" style. An ancient style of shrine architecture, it is believed to be of "heaven-earth" origin, that is, divinely inspired. The Grand Shrine at Ise is in Mei Province.*

shrines. Worship there is the highest expression of respect to the emperor, the country, and all Japanese culture as well as to Amaterasu. Pilgrims travel there for prayer and spiritual renewal; a pilgrimage to Ise connects the Japanese to the kami power that founded their nation. They buy paper talismans to take back to their kamidana, carrying the blessing of the sun goddess into their homes.

Other Shrines

Famous and beautiful shrines of all kinds dot Japan. Many have great national significance. One of these is the Yasukuni Shrine in Tokyo. This is a special shrine for war dead, who were

believed to become kami when they gave their lives for their country. During the time of State Shinto, the Yasukuni Shrine was one of the largest and most influential in the nation, and it is still prized for its historical significance.

The Meiji Shrine commemorates Emperor Meiji, and other great emperors have shrines dedicated to them as well. On the coast of Honshu opposite Ise is the shrine of Izumo, where Susanowo fought with the serpent. An ancient shrine, it is believed to stand on the site where Susanowo's descendant, Oho-kuni-nushi, had his palace, and where Ninigi first took control of the country.

In Toyokawa, the shrine to Inari draws huge crowds. Inari, once a Buddhist god of rice harvest, is now associated with success in business. The shrine is part of a Buddhist temple complex, reflecting the time when Buddhist grounds included Shinto shrines. Huge crowds throng the festivals there, especially the New Year's Festival, to enjoy the festivities and pray for success in business and for prosperity.

The shrine of Itsukushima is dedicated to the sea kami. Its torii rise from the water at high tide. The shrine of Kasuga stands in deep woods where deer, the messengers of that kami, wander freely. These and other such shrines emphasize the closeness and power of nature.

Some shrines specialize in a particular kind of blessing. A seashore shrine, for example, might offer the blessing of good fishing. Students visit the shrine of kami associated with good grades at exam time. Often, people who are seeking marriage visit shrines associated with *ryoen*, making good marriages, and *enmusubi*, linking people together as a couple. The Izumo Shrine is popular with couples and with singles seeking partners. During his long transformation from troublemaker to benefactor, Susanowo became associated with love and now receives petitions for suitable matches. Another such shrine is the Jishu Shrine in Kyoto. A leaflet handed out by the shrine praises family life and marriage, and says, in part, "There are still many things in this world that are unattainable through human power alone. At such times how grateful we are that we can depend on the power of the kami to eliminate all the hindrances…"

Some shrines attract visitors and tourists because of their well-kept grounds and interesting histories. Others receive pilgrims, individuals who make a pledge to the kami to visit a particular shrine or a group of shrines. Devotees may try to visit as many of Japan's more than 80,000 shrines as they can.

The Importance of Sacred Spaces

Sacred spaces for the Japanese are not limited to special buildings, like synagogues, churches, or mosques. Sacred spaces can be found wherever there are kami. There are kami in great rocks and enormous trees, in the thresholds, kitchens, fireplaces, and kami-shelves of homes, in the villages of fishermen, and on the ships of sailors, making all these and many more places sacred spaces, too. Additional sacred spaces include those places where babies have been born or where they celebrate their birth rituals or coming-of-age rites. They are also the beautiful grounds of shrines where marriages are celebrated. Sacred spaces are everywhere the kami are, and the kami inhabit every corner of Japan. They are the sacred spiritual powers informing Japan's lands, its people, and its government.

The Japanese people constantly need to recall that every corner of their homeland and every aspect of their cultural life has a further spiritual dimension. They must see this if they are to be truly aware and appreciative of the bounty of nature and the unpredictable character of good and bad fortune. They are always conscious of the blessings of the kami from whom all things come, and they are continually aware of the rhythms of life that are marked by good and bad times. Even if they are not religious, the Japanese people derive a strong spiritual dimension from their Shinto traditions. This enables them to draw joy and spiritual refreshment from the land and sea that surround them, from the homes and families that nourish them, and from remembered and venerated ancestors who, through example, inspire them continually to develop courage, determination, and strength. Shinto values pulse through all that they do.

CHAPTER 9

Shinto Today

When one knows the nature and history of Shinto, it is difficult to imagine it surviving in the modern world. Shinto has been so tied to a simple agrarian lifestyle—with its natural rhythms, its kami of farms and woodlands, and its center in family life—that one can hardly picture it having a role in an urban industrial setting. Its preservation seemed guaranteed more than a century ago only because Japan had chosen to keep itself cut off from the developing Western industrial world.

Today, Japan is one of the world's strongest industrial nations. Upon the ruins of World War II, modern Japan rebuilt itself into a country of active, thriving cities and commerce. Its factories competed throughout the world, challenging the chief car-exporting countries of the West, replacing American and European firms as leaders in the field of electronics, exporting appliances throughout the globe, and sharing the lead in technology with the great industrial countries of the world.

Shinto has traditionally played a twofold role in Japanese society. First, it has helped members of families to find meaning in life and, with the aid of the kami, to meet the challenges they

Preceding page-
Mount Fuji, or
Fujiyama, Japan's
highest and most
famous peak, and the
home of the kami
Sengen Sama, draws
hundreds of thousands
of pilgrims each year.

face in all the different areas of their existence. This first role has been the concern of religious Shinto from its earliest days. Secondly, Shinto has also nurtured in the Japanese people a feeling of solidarity and has attempted to unite all Japanese as citizens of a larger national society. This effort has been supported by traditional religious Shinto and by State Shinto, the nonreligious form of Shinto that treated its members as followers of a cultural, rather than a religious, tradition.

Shinto in Postwar Japan

After World War II, the forces of Occupation ordered the Japanese government to cut all ties with Shinto shrines. This was the way they believed nationalism and worship of the emperor would be weakened and eventually eradicated. No public funds could be used to support Shinto shrines. The government attempted to preserve Shinto tradition by declaring State Shinto to be cultural, not religious. In this way, the Japanese people could continue many of their traditions. Visits to shrines, however, waned, and Shinto festivals diminished. To continue the disappearing religious dimensions of Shinto, some Japanese, to meet their spiritual needs, quietly switched to Buddhism. Others joined the New Religions of Sect Shinto that had developed to adapt Shinto to the modern world and its demands.

The war, however, had changed Japanese life appreciably. As the people attempted to rebuild their homeland, they inexorably pursued opportunities available in the offices and factories of the growing cities. Once again, but much more dramatically, the people lost contact with the agricultural rhythms that have been the foundation of the Shinto way of life. Not only did they lose contact with the shrines of their rural backgrounds, they also lost, more and more, their tight bonds to the families that had preserved their Shinto religious roots. Likewise, city life divorced people from the natural life of the rural areas that had continually acknowledged the presence of kami. In the bustling cities, fewer homes had kamidana, and many religious ceremonies were no longer celebrated. Sacred ceremonies were reduced to purely secular celebrations.

The Peace Constitution of 1946

Although the Peace Constitution of 1946 guaranteed freedom of religion, it also ordered the Japanese government to sever all ties with Shinto shrines and forbade the use of public funds to support these shrines. While this was a serious blow to Shrine Shinto, private support of the people became strong, and the Association of Shrine Shinto was formed to rebuild ruined shrines and to revive religious practices. More than 80,000 shrines, of various sizes, now exist in Japan. Some of the larger ones, which have become tourist attractions, are secular in character and are administered by government appointees. Others are religious shrines where many Japanese, weary from the hustle and bustle of modern commercial life, seek spiritual refreshment through their Shinto ritual traditions.

The tensions between those who want to preserve the traditional religious dimensions of Shinto and those who wish for a more secular interpretation of Shinto traditions are very strong.

■ *Foundations of Shrine Shinto*

The association of Shrine Shinto, formed after World War II, sets forth its goals for modern Shinto in three principles:

1. *To express gratitude for divine favor and the benefits of ancestors, and with a bright, pure, sincere mind to devote ourselves to the shrine rites and festivals.*

2. *To serve society and others and, in the realization of ourselves as divine messengers, to endeavor to improve and consolidate the world.*

3. *To identify our minds with the emperor's mind and, in loving and being friendly with one another, to pray for the country's prosperity and for the peaceful coexistence and co-prosperity for the people of the world.*

from Shinto, the Kami Way, by Sokyo Ono.

The case of the Yasukuni Shrine is a good example of these tensions. This shrine is a memorial to those who died defending the emperor and the nation, and as religious heroes they have been

■ The seven-day New Year's Festival is the most important event of the Shinto year. More than one hundred thousand Japanese visit their shrines at this time to make offerings and pray for prosperity in the coming year. Here, Iwashimizu Shrine at Kyoto, Japan, is thronged with New Year's visitors.

elevated to the level of kami. It was a great honor to be enshrined at Yasukuni as a person of religious dedication to one's country. Yasukuni is both a shrine and a war memorial. As a religious shrine, support for it is forbidden. As a war memorial, many military leaders and the families of those who died in war have lobbied to nationalize the shrine. Opposing this measure are those who fear the revival of the kind of intense nationalism that marked the identification of the state and Shinto religion.

Religious Festivals in a Secular Age

The Peace Constitution of 1946 forced government officials at every level to avoid public support of religion. One way of fulfilling this requirement has been to turn the traditional religious festivals into cultural events that draw crowds of tourists. The

festivals have become secular events that bring people back to nature, put them in touch again with kami, and promote harmony and unity among the participants. Since these festivals include religious rituals, religious participants enjoy spiritual renewal, whereas non-religious participants share in the joy and warmth of cultural remembrances.

Cultural celebrations often draw people on the basis of their renown. Advertising and promotions tend to entice crowds to the national shrines, such as Meiji in Tokyo, Sumiyoshi in Osaka, Atsuta in Nagoya, and Fushimi Inari in Kyoto. At these popular shrines, visitors often number in the millions. Smaller local shrines tend to draw lesser numbers, but the participants are distinctly religious, who pursue visits that are much more marked by prayer and meditation.

Cultural and Religious Pilgrimages

As Americans might visit Yosemite Park, the Grand Canyon, or the Liberty Bell, so many Japanese plan their vacations around the more than 80,000 shrines throughout Japan. Many tourists are courted by the advertising of famous shrines or of those in scenic areas. Some shrines have large collections of art that make them equivalent to museums. Others offer lessons in national pride that supplement family outings and picnics. Many of the smaller shrines in rural areas, now quite depopulated by the exodus to the cities, sell charms for luck, or memorabilia, or offer tours for visitors.

In contrast to these cultural excursions, however, modern Shinto believers also make pilgrimages. They may choose to visit a group of shrines or a particular shrine repeatedly to show special respect to the kami of that shrine. Often, they make their pilgrimages on foot, walking from shrine to shrine in a spirit of special devotion. At times, urban Shinto believers will visit their favorite shrine before work or during lunchtime.

Shinto in the World of Big Business

The Shinto values of honesty, cooperation, loyalty, and unified effort are very much prized by Japanese businesses. With the great migration of people from the village to the larger cities, companies have taken over the role of village, encouraging workers to imagine themselves as parts of an extended corporate family. People are hired for a position in a company very much as if they are joining a family. It's as if they are told, "This business will be your home for life."

Shinto ideals are inculcated from birth and set the tone for a workplace that is envied by manufacturers throughout the world. Western companies study the methods of cooperation, teamwork, and loyalty in Japanese businesses, to try to improve production in their own worlds.

The companies have gone beyond pursuing Shinto ideals. They imitate Shinto practices by constructing their own office buildings and setting up altars where they pray for assistance and make offerings to the building kami. Businesses have at times even erected shrines in their office buildings to provide a quiet place of beauty for nonreligious staff and a spiritual home to facilitate devotions for those who want to observe them.

The Challenge of the New Religions

From the perspectives of the new religions, the thirteen denominations classified as Sect Shinto during the State Shinto period stand in contrast to the established mainstream Japanese religions, Shinto and Buddhism. The established religions were viewed as institutionalized and grounded on the social setting of the household rather than on individual faith and commitment. They are portrayed by the new religions as hierarchical, bureaucratic, and out of touch with the lives and spiritual needs of ordinary individuals.

It is important to keep this portrait of the established religions in mind in order to understand the appeal of the new religions. They represent themselves as a confident and continuing effort to provide an individually based faith that would be relevant to individual believers in their everyday life. Joining a new religion is at first a matter of conversion and personal faith, not a matter of social circumstances. The general tendency among the new religions is to think of the older new religions as tending to become stale and routine. The older new religions often lose members to the newer and more dynamic groups.

The Sect Shinto groups were suppressed, or at least discouraged, when State Shinto was obligatory, but with the Peace Constitution's guarantee of freedom of religion, they have attracted many followers. Each new religion tends more to reinterpret and to provide an alternative reformulation of extant religions rather than to present new ideas. They make what already exists more relevant for people in contemporary society. New religions tend either to focus on the declarations of their founders as divine messages and their writings as revealed scriptures, or, if they are connected to Buddhism, to base their reforms on particular texts from the Buddhist canon.

No matter the source of their inspiration, the new religions stress the importance of ancestral spirits and believe that misfortunes are spiritual trials that require religious and ritual solutions. Through techniques learned in the new religion and through the grace of its leaders and kami, people can find liberation, solve their problems, and have a happy life. The new religions are religions of this world—they have an attitude that is positive and supportive, often asserting that the aim of existence is to live a good, happy, and positive life here on Earth. The new religions are religions for people who have lost their natural communities and want to belong to a group of like-minded people. It is their way of recreating a community feeling.

The Enduring Vitality of Shrine Shinto

Many Japanese sense that a great deal of their spiritual heritage has been buried under the pressures of the secularization that dominates modern society. They see cultural Shinto as totally nonreligious. They view the new religions as competitors for the hearts and minds of those who want their religion to be relevant. Religious Shinto, however, has always found ways to adapt. It has adapted to the challenges of Confucianism, Taoism, and Buddhism throughout its history. More recently it has kept its identity despite the challenges of State Shinto.

As their shrines began to fall into ruin when State Shinto was forbidden to support their upkeep and repair, the believing Shinto community raised money to refurbish them. When deserted villages left few people to pray to the kami of the rice

■ *Religious Shinto has refurbished many shrines that had fallen into ruin. Here, a Shinto woman believer prays at a restored shrine.*

harvest, or when fishermen deserted their boats and neglected the kami of the sea, the Shinto faithful in the cities discovered new kami—the kami of businesses. Shinto believers discovered new kami in the many new arenas of their lives. Students made pilgrimages to Tenmanju shrines to ask the kami of study to help them get good grades. Athletes at the Winter Olympics at Sapphora prayed to the kami of the mountains to give them victory in their contests. Business men visited shrines before work and appealed to the kami to bring them financial prosperity.

It is true that many shrines have become centers of tourism and that the festivals held there are often cultural. Yet not all who participate in these rituals are bereft of religion. Some people participate with a true Shinto religious spirit. For them, religious ceremonies are religious. Their appeals to the kami are sincere. Their Shinto faith is still alive.

Shinto, the Spiritual Roots of Japanese Culture

It is in the Shinto festivals that the heart of Japan can be seen. Shinto is judged at times not to be a religion because it has neither scriptures nor saints. Yet the Latin *ligare,* one of the roots of the word *religion*, means "to bind," and Shinto is a binding force within society. Japanese religion is based on feelings rather than doctrines, and these feelings are best revealed in the celebration of festivals where the Japanese people reveal their contact with the divine in its simpler aspects. In these acts of celebration the Japanese people reveal their spiritual view of nature and their deep reverence for their ancestors. In both cases, the festival participants reveal their sense of dependence on natural forces beyond themselves in all the activities they perform throughout the year. They also acknowledge their indebtedness to their ancestors for giving them the gift of life and all the benefits that allow them to enjoy it. Along with this sense of dependence is the awareness of the need for thanksgiving that they should be expressing to their kami. Awareness of dependency and gratitude for the various gifts of life are central attitudes for the Shinto way of life.

This fundamental Shinto approach to life is revealed most of all in the family, which is the backbone of society. Children become aware of how parents protect and care for them, and they realize that they can never repay the debt they owe to their parents. They also learn that the interest of the family is more important than that of the individual. These are lessons not learned from books or lectures, but from the lived experience of how the family functions and celebrates its connection to others and how the family expresses its gratitude to all the kami that have brought special benefits to it.

A similar set of attitudes is developed in the collection of families called a village. This is the natural extension of family life that manifests further dependence on other families for assistance and support in all the endeavors of human life. For this help, the Shinto families all express their gratitude to those who surround them. This extends further to regional and national dependency and gratitude and builds a cohesiveness and spirit of cooperation among all the Japanese people.

Shinto has been preserved not by doctrines but by experiences in the family, the village, the region, and the whole of Japanese society. Those experiences mirror the basic attitudes of Japanese culture. Japanese society is based on natural groupings, such as the family and the village, rather than on groups centered in education, occupations, or individual preferences. Even as these natural settings have been tainted by modern alterations of life, the culture of the Japanese is so rooted in its Shinto past that companies and businesses follow the rhythms of the family and village as they develop. They are directed by the Shinto values of honesty, cooperation, loyalty, and unity of effort. Shinto is the very basis of Japanese culture.

GLOSSARY

Association of Shrine Shinto— Organization that oversees Shinto shrines, the Shinto priesthood, and the calendar of religious festivals in modern Japan.

Chigi—Characteristic crossed end-beams of the roof of some Shinto shrines.

Daimyo—Nobles who administered large land holdings and peasants during feudal times under the shoguns.

Doka—"Poetry of the way," religious tanka, especially that written by Kurozumi Munetada, founder of Kurozumi Shinto.

Engishiki—Collection of ancient Shinto myths.

Folk Shinto—Ancient form of Shinto on which most modern Shinto practices are based.

Gohei—Symbolic offering to the kami; a wand hung with folded strips of white paper.

Ikigami—Living kami.

Imperial Household Shinto—Shinto worship carried on by the emperor as chief priest.

Ise—Location of the shrine complex dedicated to Amaterasu and containing the Naiku shrine, most sacred of all Shinto shrines.

Kagura—Sacred Shinto dances performed during the Shinto ceremonies and festivals.

Kami—A god or gods worshiped in Shinto, who represented natural phenomena or mythological ancestors such as Amaterasu, the sun goddess.

Kamidana—Shinto kami-shelf, or altar, usually found in the home.

Kojiki—Record of Ancient Matters, thought to be written in 712 C.E. and recording the mythological origins of Japan and the imperial line.

Matsuri—Term for a Shinto festival.

Meiji—Emperor whose rule began in 1868 and whose policies ushered in Japan's technological growth, interaction with Western powers, and development of State Shinto.

Meiji Restoration—Period beginning with Meiji's rule during which power was restored to the emperor from the shoguns. Shinto was separated from Buddhism and given prominence as the established state religion.

Miko—Shrine maiden; a young woman who performs ritual dances and other shrine duties.

Mikoshi—A palanquin (chest) on long poles, in which the kami are symbolically carried around a town during a festival.

Miyamairi—Presentation of a newborn child to the family's local shrine.

New Religions—Religious movements, some based on Shinto and others on Buddhism, that were classified as Sect Shinto during the Meiji period.

Nihongi (also **Nihon Shoki**)—Chronicles of Ancient Japan, completed in the eighth century, recording the traditions of Shinto and the kami from prehistoric times.

Norito (also **Norii**)—Ancient prayers used by priests in Shinto ceremonies.

Oharai—The norito, or prayer, of the Great Purification ritual.

Polytheistic—Having many deities, characteristic of Shinto.

Ryobu Shinto—So-called double-aspect Shinto that associated Shinto deities with Buddhist gods.

Sakaki—Sacred tree of Shinto. It is widely planted on shrine grounds and its branches are sometimes used in Shinto purification rites.

Samurai—Japanese warrior class in feudal times.

Sando—The approach to a shrine.

Sect Shinto—New Religions, or religious sects classified by the Meiji government.

Shichigosan—The annual seven-five-three festival, a day of prayer for the welfare of children, when boys of five and girls of three and seven visit their shrine.

Shintai—A sacred symbol of kami, such as the mirror enshrined at Ise, which is the shintai of Amaterasu.

Shinto—Japanese religion that developed from prehistoric folk religions, featuring the worship of kami.

Shogun—Military dictator. Shoguns ruled Japan from the end of the twelfth century to 1867.

Shrine—Shinto sacred building where kami are enshrined and prayers are offered.

Shrine Shinto (Jinja honcho)—A form of Shinto in which priests performed rites as if kami were present.

State Shinto—A nonreligious form of Shinto, made obligatory during the Meiji Restoration and banned after World War II.

Tenrikyo—A religion founded by Miki Nakayama in 1838, based on Shinto. It was the first of the New Religions to gain many followers and is still attracting adherents.

Tokugawa Period—A period of strict rule by Tokugawa shoguns, 1603–1864.

Torii—Sacred gateway to a Shinto shrine.

Tutelary Kami—Guardian kami of local shrines; the kami that protect people living in a given area.

Uji—Clan

Yamato—Geographical area south of Nara in central Japan; clan from which the imperial line emerged.

Yasukuni—Tokyo shrine that enshrines war dead as kami.

Zen—Form of Buddhism widely practiced in Japan.

CHAPTER NOTES

page 19　　"Come out and see,…" from the *Kojiki*, as translated in *Asiatic Mythology*, by J. Hacklin and Clement Huart.

page 24　　"Consider…forever," from the *Kojiki*, as translated in *Asiatic Mythology*, by J. Hacklin and Clement Huart.

page 44　　Buddha's Four Noble Truths from *World Religions: Buddhism*, by Madhu Bazaz Wangu.

page 68　　"The Imperial rule…one roof," as quoted in *Religions of Japan*, by H. Byron Earhart.

page 110　"There are still many things… " Jinju Shrine (Kyoto) leaflet, quoted in *Religion in Contemporary Japan*, by Ian Reader.

FOR FURTHER READING

Blumberg, Rhoda. *Commodore Perry in the Land of the Shogun*, 2nd ed. New York: HarperCollins Publishers, 2002.

Holtom, Daniel C. *The National Faith of Japan: A Study in Modern Shinto (The Kegan Paul Japan Library*, Vol. 1). London/New York: Kegan Paul International, 1996.

Langone, John. *In the Shogun's Shadow: Understanding a Changing Japan*. Boston: Little, Brown and Company, 1994.

Nelson, John. *Enduring Identities: The Guise of Shinto in Contemporary Japan*. Honolulu: University of Hawai'i Press, 2000.

Ono, Sokyo. *Shinto: The Kami Way*. Rutland, Vt./Tokyo: Charles E. Tuttle Co., Inc., 1994.

Picken, Stuart D. B. *Essentials of Shinto: An Analytical Guide to Principal Teachings*. Westport/London: Greenwood Publishing Group, 1994.

Tames, Richard. *Passport to Japan*, 2nd ed. Danbury, Conn.: Franklin Watts, Inc., 1997.

INDEX